GETTING EVEN

GETTING EVEN

Forgiveness and Its Limits

Jeffrie G. Murphy

UNIVERSITY PRESS

2003

OXFORD
UNIVERSITY PRESS

Oxford   New York
Auckland   Bangkok   Buenos Aires   Cape Town   Chennai
Dar es Salaam   Delhi   Hong Kong   Istanbul   Karachi   Kolkata
Kuala Lumpur   Madrid   Melbourne   Mexico City   Mumbai   Nairobi
São Paulo   Shanghai   Taipei   Tokyo   Toronto

Copyright © 2003 by Oxford University Press, Inc.

Published by Oxford University Press, Inc.
198 Madison Avenue, New York, New York 10016

www.oup.com

Library of Congress Cataloging-in-Publication Data
Murphy, Jeffrie G.
Getting even : forgiveness and its limits / by Jeffrie G. Murphy.
p. cm.
Includes bibliographical references and index.
ISBN 0-19-515149-6
1. Forgiveness. I. Title.
BF637.F67 M87 2003
155.9'2—dc 21   2002034622

1 3 5 7 9 8 6 4 2

Printed in the United States of America
on acid-free paper

For Lee and James Canacakos—
inlaws who enrich my family life,
and
James Weinstein—
friend, colleague, and constant source
of intellectual stimulation.

PREFACE

Understand and forgive, my mother said, and the effort has quite exhausted me. I could do with some anger to energize me, and bring me back to life again. But where can I find that anger? Who is to help me? My friends? I have been understanding and forgiving my friends, my female friends, for as long as I can remember. . . . Understand and forgive. . . . Understand husbands, wives, fathers, mothers. Understand dog fights above and the charity box below, understand fur-coated women and children without shoes. Understand school—Jonah, Job, and the nature of the Deity; understand Hitler and the bank of England and the behavior of Cinderella's sisters. Preach acceptance to wives and tolerance to husbands. . . . Grit your teeth, endure. Understand, forgive, accept, in the light of your own death, your own inevitable corruption. . . .

Oh mother, what you taught me! And what a miserable, crawling, snivelling way to go, the worn-out slippers placed neatly beneath the bed, careful not to give offense.

Fay Weldon, *Female Friends*

When told of Truman Capote's death, Gore Vidal is said to have responded: "Good career move."

My own decision, in the late eighties, to begin writing on forgiveness has proven a good if less final career move for me. Up until that time, I had, like most professional philosophers, published material that either appealed to a very small academic audience of fellow philosophers or—even worse and to use Hume's phrase—"fell deadborn from the press," read, so far as I could tell, by nobody at all. My work on for-giveness, however, gained attention not merely in philosophy but also in such other academic fields as law, theology, and clinical psychology; and it even, to a welcome degree, appealed to a nonacademic audience. So I began to receive invitations—continuing to this day—to present lectures on forgiveness to groups of various kinds, academic and nonacademic, and to write more on the topic.

Since, like most academics, I am driven to a nontrivial degree by vanity (there is little money in what I do), I cannot say that I was indif-ferent to this positive attention. For I hope more honorable reasons, I particularly welcomed the fact that I was sometimes reaching, even with writings aimed primarily at academics, a nonacademic audience. It is gratifying to think that one's ideas might matter outside the confines of one's own little club.

What was the reason for this comparative success? I think it was based primarily on two facts: (1) Forgiveness was and is a very "in" topic (just take twelve steps over to the self-help and recovery section of any bookstore and you will find the word "forgiveness" in a great many of the titles) and (2) I was one of the few voices that was to any degree *neg-ative* on the value of forgiveness—thereby bucking a trendy and almost messianic sentimental movement that sees forgiveness as a nearly uni-versal panacea for all mental, moral, and spiritual ills. (Even physical ills! A book was recently published—I kid you not—where the author ar-gues that people who forgive will live longer and be more free of disease than those who do not forgive.)

Because in my writing I tended to stress objections to forgiveness and to raise cautions about it, some people came to see me—wrongly—as an enemy of forgiveness. Indeed, a colleague, when he heard that I was writing (with Jean Hampton) a book with the title *Forgiveness and Mercy,* asked me if the subtitle of the book was going to be "An Out-sider's View." Although his question may have been based in part on his perception of me as a fairly vindictive and unforgiving person, it was no doubt at least in part also based on his interpretation of some of my writings on the topic.

The purpose of this book is to present for the educated and serious general reader—in a nontechnical and nonscholarly form (no foot-notes, for example)—a concise general outline of my present thinking on the topic of forgiveness. At the end of the book I provide a brief bib-liography listing the writings on which I have drawn most heavily—my own writings and the writings of others. This book will involve some compression and simplification not present in my more academic writings, and readers who would welcome a discussion of all the complexities may consult those writings. In spite of the noted compression and simplification, however, this book does not seek to condescend. Indeed, as the book progresses, certain topics are discussed in some depth. What I have tried to eliminate is not the depth and seriousness of discussion but rather the kind of tangents that could be of interest only to academic specialists.

I will (perhaps to the surprise of some) have much to say in favor of forgiveness and will indeed endorse it in many circumstances. I will also, however, continue my attempt to offer objections to forgiveness and to counsel cautions with respect to its hasty adoption as a response to wrongdoing. In my view such a response risks compromising some very important values—for example, self-respect.

We all know the cliché that "to err is human; to forgive, divine," but I think we also need to recall S. J. Perelman's variation on this cliché: "To err is human; to forgive, supine." The message of this book is that the truth lies somewhere between these two extremes.

Many people, of course, tend to locate forgiveness in a religious context and to see forgiveness as essentially a religious—perhaps particularly Christian—virtue. Such an assumption might lead some readers to expect this book to take the form of a sermon, and perhaps to some degree this will be the case. Sermons are generally based on a text, however, and—since some of my sermon will be negative—I have taken as my opening text a very negative passage on forgiveness from the writer Fay Weldon. The passage, which I also quoted in the first book I published on the topic, should set an opening tone in marked contrast to the uncritical upbeat boosterism that one finds in most contemporary writings on forgiveness.

I will, in the final chapters of the book, consider with sympathy the Christian case in favor of forgiveness and in the process reveal some of my own religious commitments. I prefer, however, that the good news come after the bad news has been fully digested and appreciated.

Tempe, Arizona
November 2002

ACKNOWLEDGMENTS

I would like to thank Peter Ohlin, my editor at Oxford University Press, for his encouragement of this project and my colleague Professor Michael White for reading and commenting on large portions of the manuscript. I also thank again all those whom I have previously thanked in my earlier works on forgiveness and related issues. In particular, I want to pay respects to the memory of the late Jean Hampton with whom I co-authored my first book on the topic. Finally, I thank my wife Ellen Canacakos. She has as usual had both a direct and indirect effect on my work—bringing her intelligence to bear in helping me to improve some of the chapters and reminding me, in so many ways, that her supportive presence is one of the few unambiguously good things that has ever happened in my life. Without her, I probably could not be bothered—with this or with anything else.

CONTENTS

Introduction: Responding to Evil   3

1 What Is Forgiveness?   9

2 Two Cheers for Vindictiveness   17

3 Vindictiveness and the Law   27

4 Forgiveness as a Virtue   33

5 Repentance, Punishment, and Mercy   39

6 Self-Forgiveness   57

7 Forgiveness in Psychotheraphy   73

8 Forgiveness and Christianity   87

9 Christianity and Criminal Punishment   95

Concluding Remarks   115

Further Reading   119

Index   125

GETTING EVEN

RESPONDING TO EVIL

I will frame my discussion by asking a question that requires honest introspection of anyone who tries to answer it. The question is this: Suppose that I am a victim of *evil*—of violent crime, state torture, or other serious wrongdoing. What kind of victim should I try to be—a vindictive victim perhaps seeking vengeance or a forgiving victim perhaps seeking reconciliation?

Being wronged by others does not always engage this question, of course, because sometimes our response to being wronged is more a sense of hurt or disappointment or deep sadness rather than a temptation to strike back or otherwise get even. Perhaps there are even interesting gender differences here. In the area in which I do most of my scholarly work, however—the philosophy of criminal law and its related emotions—getting even is a central issue. Vindictiveness, temptations to revenge, and struggles to channel or even overcome these passions are always on the table—particularly in criminal sentencing and in parole, pardon, and clemency hearings. It is this tension that I hope to be able to illuminate a bit—at least to provide a philosophical overview or framework in which intellectual discussion of the tension can be structured.

Because, perhaps, much of American society pays at least lip service to Judeo-Christianity, that society also pays at least lip service to the idea that forgiveness is an important moral value. And yet Americans generally seem to support unusually harsh mechanisms of criminal punishment—for example, America is the only Western democracy that retains capital punishment and tends to impose prison sentences of a length and severity that most Western democracies find excessive. To what degree, if at all, are these punitive practices consistent with our professed commitments to such values as love, mercy, and forgiveness? Consider also the current cultural phenomenon often referred to as "the victims' rights movement." This is seen by many Europeans simply as evidence of the out-of-control vindictiveness of American society in general. The justice of the rule of law is, in the view of many foreign and domestic critics of the movement, being perverted by such practices as the presentation of highly charged and angry victim impact statements—statements that cloud reason and may emotionally sway judges or juries toward much harsher sentences than some criminals deserve.

Supporters of the movement, of course, see it merely as giving crime victims a place in a legal process that has for too long treated them as outsiders. And if you say to them "What about forgiveness?" they reply that there is plenty of room for forgiveness for *victims who want to forgive* but that there should also be a voice given to victims who do not want to forgive but who prefer to get even. Victim impact statements allow both sorts of victims to play a role in influencing the sentence, and this—according to supporters of the movement—is all to the good.

We are often torn, when considering revenge versus forgiveness, by a deep tension between competing values—for example, the expected satisfaction of getting even versus the belief that the virtuous person should be loving and forgiving, not vindictive. This tension may leave a person unfulfilled whatever course of action is taken—perhaps feeling guilty if revenge is indeed taken, perhaps feeling weak and servile if it is not.

We also tend to find the nature and scope of the values themselves somewhat hard to understand. Is revenge-taking inconsistent with justice, or is legal justice perhaps nothing more than institutionalized revenge? If legal punishment is different from revenge, then one may legitimately seek it for a wrongdoer without being charged with vindictiveness. If legal punishment is not different from revenge, however, then—unless one wants to abandon legal punishment—one might want to blunt one's criticism of vindictiveness. (Shortly after September 11, 2001, President Bush said that we should seek justice and not vengeance. But is there really a difference?) If we decide to consider forgiveness as an option for responding to evil, then we are still faced with some puzzles—for example, should forgiveness be bestowed as a free gift without any pre-conditions or should it be contingent on sincere repentance on the part of the wrongdoer?

I plan in this book to explore some of these issues—to present a philosophical overview in terms of which discussion of the question "How ought one to respond to evil?" might profitably be structured. I will explore the nature and value of revenge ("getting even"), the nature and value of forgiveness, the nature and value of repentance, and the role that religious values might legitimately play in all this. I will discuss these issues not merely as issues of personal morality but also in the context of such important social practices as criminal punishment and psychotherapy—discussing, in the context of the latter, the issue of self-forgiveness.

Before doing any of this, however, there are three preliminary points I would like to make.

First, I should note that most of my thinking and writing on forgiveness and reconciliation has concerned what might be called *interpersonal forgiveness* and reconciliation—for example, forgiveness of an unfaithful spouse, a betraying friend, a malicious colleague, a government agent by whom one has been tortured, or, most centrally, a criminal by whom one has been victimized. With respect to law, my focus has been more on criminal than private law.

Those interested in what might be called *group forgiveness* will, I hope, find what I say here a useful start, but for a detailed discussion of such things as truth commissions (e.g., South Africa's Truth and Reconciliation Commission) they must look elsewhere—for example, at Martha Minow's fine book *Between Vengeance and Forgiveness: Facing History after Genocide and Mass Violence*. I will, for example, sometimes discuss South Africa's commission in passing, to illustrate a particular point, but I make no pretense that such discussion will do justice to the detailed complexity of the issues raised by that commission.

The second preliminary point I want to make—a personal one—concerns my own qualifications to speak on the topic in question. I have been thinking and writing about this topic for many years, and over the years I have developed increasingly positive views about the value of forgiveness. However, I want to make it clear that my current views are essentially intellectual and theoretical rather than autobiographical in nature. Although I have over the years suffered my share of petty slights and insults, I have led an astoundingly fortunate life in the realm of victimization. I have experienced some small-scale immorality, but nothing that I would identify as *evil*. I have never to my knowledge been betrayed by a loved one or friend; I have never been tortured; I have never been raped; I have never been violently assaulted or been the victim of any crime more serious than auto theft—nor has anyone close to me. Thus, when I later speak of forgiveness as a virtue, I know that I may be open to the charge "Easy for you to say." When those who have been seriously victimized can emerge from their victimization without hate and with their self-respect intact, we may see nobility and moral grandeur in their capacity to forgive. Nelson Mandela seems to be such a person. I have no idea, however, if I could rise to this in similar circumstances; and thus I will express my admiration for such people without ever meaning to suggest that I know that I could act in a comparable way.

The third and final preliminary point I want to make concerns the level of precision that one can expect on the topic of forgiveness. With Aristotle, I tend to think that it is generally a mistake in ethics to aim for a level of precision not really allowed by what is in fact a quite messy and conflicted subject matter. Neat formal theories in ethics generally produce not illumination but rather (in Herbert Hart's fine phrase) uniformity at the price of distortion. I am convinced, indeed, that a really insightful book on ethics would not have as a title "The Theory of . . . " but rather something like "Muddling Through" or "Stumbling Along."

Philosophy is, after all, a strange discipline. When I tell people I do philosophy, a certain look comes into their eyes. I do not like this look, although I think that I understand it. Unlike many academic subjects, philosophy does not settle things for us by adding to our store of factual knowledge. In this way, it is not like history, or mathematics, or science. And because it does not settle anything, it often disappoints people—a disappointment that can easily lead to the suspicion that philosophy has no value at all.

The philosopher John Wisdom conveyed in this way his own feelings of despair at the dismissive attitude he sensed that others sometimes direct toward philosophy:

> Scientists don't have to feel like this. They tell us what we don't know until they tell us—how very fast germs in the blood breed and that this stuff will stop them, what will or at least won't take the stain out of the carpet. Even if I were a historian it would be better. Maybe you don't want to know just how the abbey at Bury St. Edmunds was run at the time of the Abbot Samson, but at least you probably don't know and if only I did I could tell you. (Wisdom, 1964, p. 275)

But if philosophy is not like this, what is its value? At its best, it does what Richard Rorty calls *advancing the conversation*—generally, in Socratic fashion, going against the grain of conventional wisdom and raising more questions than it answers. In ethics, philosophy does not provide new ethical truths but rather tries to assist us in thinking more clearly about ethical or moral issues. It does this by clarifying concepts—defining terms if you prefer—and exposing (and forcing us to bring to consciousness) the hard value choices and conflicts at the core of our moral lives.

On the present topic of forgiveness, for example: we cannot even begin to discuss intelligently the value of forgiveness until we have at least a reasonably clear understanding of what forgiveness is. Otherwise we shall be like those poor fellows in the Lewis Carroll poem who find it a great obstacle to their snark hunt that they do not know what a snark is.

Once we have at least a provisional understanding of forgiveness, we may begin to see the ways it might be in conflict with other values—self-respect and self-defense, for example. Seeing such a potential conflict, we have several options: decide simply to live with it ("consistency is the hobgoblin of small minds"), seek to remove it by rethinking the concepts of forgiveness or self-respect in such a way that they are rendered consistent, or decide to rank our values so that some are allowed to trump others—for example, "I will forgive only in circumstances where I can do so without sacrificing my self-respect—for example, by forgiving only the truly repentant."

Philosophy can lay all this out, but it cannot settle things. It cannot resolve the various conflicts that now lie exposed. It cannot develop a formal decision procedure for forgiveness—some method of proving, for example, that you ought or ought not rank self-respect higher than forgiveness if there is indeed a conflict between the two. For this reason my discussion—like Aristotle's—will often take the form of "on the one hand, but on the other hand." This will not settle things by providing a last word, but it will at least perhaps bring it to consciousness and force us to face the fact that what the Chicago economists have told us about the economy is often true in ethics as well: there is no free lunch. Values often compete, and the pursuit of one may, as its price, involve at least the partial compromise of another.

In addition, particularly on the kinds of moral issues discussed in this book, philosophy cannot avoid being to some degree personal. Nietzsche claimed that all philosophy should be seen as a psychological autobiography of its writer, and Iris Murdoch said that the first question that should be asked of any philosopher is "What is he afraid of?"

Nietzsche and Murdoch overstate the point, but they are on to something important. Those who write on normative ethics cannot help but bring to bear perspectives drawn from their cultural, family, and religious traditions. (As the philosopher C. D. Broad put it, "we all learn our morality at our mother's knee or at some other joint.") And their own psychological natures—including their fears and hopes—will no doubt also enter the picture. This is not the whole story, of course—philosophy is not merely autobiography but must also attempt to gain rational and critical distance from all the noted factors—but the factors can never be totally escaped, particularly in forming the general perspective that selects the questions that one decides to ask and sees as central. Better to bring this to consciousness than pretend—as some philosophers do—that it is not there by claiming to speak as the voice of disembodied and unsituated reason.

There is no doubt that my original interest in the topic of forgiveness grew out of a tension I experienced in my own personality—a tension between (alas) my rather angry and even vindictive personality and my Christian upbringing, in which I had been taught the gospel of love and forgiveness. My writings on forgiveness—and my evolving views on forgiveness—have all been attempts to think clearly about this tension. I hope, of course, that many of my readers experience the same or similar tension and that they might find my own struggles with it to some degree illuminating and helpful. I can well imagine, however, that persons of a totally different nature and background might fail to be engaged at all by the way I conceive my project. Echoing the response that Eliot's Prufrock feared, some of my readers might respond to my reflections merely by saying "That is not it at all / That is not what I meant, at all."

One thing, however, I can promise: Those who would like things settled and seek a formula or decision procedure for when to forgive will not find it here. Nor will they find very many inspirational slogans. This book is not an attempt to compete with trendy psychobabble, upbeat messages on Hallmark cards, and the instant spiritual enlightenment offered on daytime talk shows. It is written for those whose primary desire is for clarity and not comfort—although it is sometimes a welcome surprise to learn how much comfort can be provided by intellectual clarity. Those old Stoics were on to something after all.

ONE

WHAT IS FORGIVENESS?

In considering possible responses to evil, I have promised a "philosophical overview" of forgiveness and related matters. Those familiar with philosophy will realize that the first thing that philosophers always do is clarify concepts—define terms, if you prefer—and draw a lot of distinctions.

There are, of course, those who like to use the phrase "*merely* a verbal matter" to dismiss such controversies as trivial, but I think that this dismissive remark is deeply mistaken. Words matter because clarity in words is a part of clarity in thinking and because some words carry great emotional and symbolic weight and thus should not be used lightly. To call someone a murderer, for example, is necessarily to condemn the person—since we do not call murderers those who kill in ways we approve. And recall the confusion generated since September 11, 2001, by sloppy uses of such terms as "vengeance," "justice," "punishment," "war," "evil," "courage," "cowardice," and "toleration." The television personality Bill Maher, for example, lost his job over his describing as courageous the terrorists that the government had already labeled as cowardly.

Thus I will begin my discussion—without apology—by trying to clarify two terms that I have so far made central: "evil" and "forgiveness." I have promised to explore forgiveness as one possible response to evil, and such exploration requires conceptual clarity. In the context of this clarification, I will draw a lot of distinctions.

Exploring in depth the nature of evil could easily consume an entire book in its own right, so I will say just enough about this concept to set the stage for my discussion of forgiveness.

What, then, is evil? It is, of course, dangerous to label any person as evil since such a label may invite one to treat that person with abandoned hatred. Such hatred may be inconsistent with a proper awareness of one's own shortcomings and with recognizing the ultimate worth of every human being—even the worst among us. Such a label also tends to demonize wrongdoers—bestowing on them a kind of aura and power that makes them seem more awesome than they in fact are. This both feeds their already pathological narcissism and tempts us to be less than rational in our response to them.

To the degree that it is useful to talk about evil, however, two aspects tend to compete for attention in our analysis of the concept—the nature of the *actions* performed and the *characters* of the persons performing those actions. Looking first at actions, we tend to think of evil in terms of the nature and gravity of the harm involved—a feature that distinguishes the evil from the merely wrong. It is wrong to break a promise, but most would probably not—except perhaps in extreme and highly unusual cases—label such an action as evil. Brutal rapes, ethnic cleansing, torture, and genocide, however, strike many as in a different moral category entirely from the merely wrong. They are paradigms of evil—of what the philosopher Robert Adams calls "moral horror." These actions seem to assault human dignity at its most fundamental level.

When we focus on character instead of actions, the paradigms of evil are—for many people—probably to be found in the realm of extreme *cruelty*—in those motives or states of character that the law of homicide (in its rather Victorian language) has called cruel, wicked, heinous, and depraved—flowing from a hardened, abandoned, and malignant heart.

But cruelty cannot be the whole story with respect to evil character. What about people who do evil because they have evil principles—principled Nazis, for example, who, like Adolf Eichmann, pride themselves on the fact that they are *not* cruel? (The person who operates the gas chambers at the animal control center may make every effort to avoid suffering to the animals that he kills. This was Eichmann's attitude toward the extermination of Jews—a frame of mind that might strike some as even worse than cruelty.) Or consider people who do evil or compromise with evil for self-interested opportunistic reasons—a good-paying job as a gas chamber operator, perhaps, or the desire to keep one's post as conductor of the Berlin Philharmonic. If we think of such people as evil or as deeply complicitous with evil, then we must admit that something other than cruelty can be essential to an evil character.

Another puzzle about evil is its relation to madness—"Mad or bad?" as the question is sometimes posed. Many of the people we are inclined to identify as evil—Charles Manson perhaps—may also strike us as quite crazy. Thus we may be torn between our desire to condemn or even hate them, on the one hand, and our belief that—being ill—they are perhaps more to be pitied than censured.

In philosophy, this puzzle has a tendency to divide the Kantians from the Aristotelians. Immanuel Kant and his followers want to make evil—even the most basic evil of character Kant calls "radical evil"—a matter of nearly total responsibility, attributable to free will all the way down.

Aristotelians, however, are more inclined to stop with character itself—identifying certain character states as virtuous and others as evil and recognizing that these states may be basic aspects of character, not because of any free choice that one has made but because of the luck of the kind of character education (habituation) experienced by the possessor. Thus, except for very extreme cases of delusional psychosis, the Aristotelian might answer the question "Bad or mad?" by saying: *both*.

Why this difference in view? The primary explanation, I think, is that Aristotle—unlike Kant—seeks to understand evil and responsibility in a rich social and political context. (Kant, on the other hand, seems to seek a secular analogue to what God might be looking for on the day of Last Judgment.) An Aristotelian will care about character as a set of traits and dispositions that make one fit (or unfit) for community membership, citizenship, and such virtuous roles as that of friend. That Aristotle holds this theory of character explains, I think, why his account of responsibility considers only factual ignorance and external compulsion as obstacles to responsibility and does not worry much about the metaphysical issue of free will versus determinism. All that matters is that one's character is fitted to one's important roles—not that one had full control over the formation of that character.

I can hardly attempt to resolve the debate between Kantians and Aristotelians in this context, but I hope that I have at least said enough to make clear that one's thinking about evil—and its relation to madness and responsibility—must be located in a larger context of value and general worldview. People do not come into the world with the label "evil" printed on their foreheads. We apply the label in accord with complex values and social practices; and to the degree that those values and practices differ, so too will the purposes for which we apply the label "evil." Given different purposes, different analyses of the concept are only to be expected.

From this brief discussion it can be seen that evil is a subject of staggering complexity—such complexity that all I can hope here is that, in a very provisional way, I have opened up the subject for further reflection. For purposes of this book I will focus for the most part on grave wrongs and harms that are inflicted maliciously or at least recklessly.

Such wrongs will of course highlight the category of evils that Robert Adams calls moral horrors—evils often arising in a criminal law context—but the discussion should not be viewed as applying only to that category. The evils most of us experience are probably not in the same league as rape or torture, but they can be very deep and in no sense trivial. Consider betrayal by a friend or spouse, for example. This is, for most normal people, a terrible wound—one that is very hard to forgive; and a book on forgiveness that had no bearing on injuries of this nature would be overly narrow.

My interest in matters of criminal law will force me often to stress evils that at least border on moral horror, but I hope that my discussion will also illuminate the wider category. With respect to those evils that tend to be the most serious crimes, I will mainly focus on this question: What is the proper response to these evils? Revenge? Legal punishment? Forgiveness? Under what circumstances, if any, are such evils ever legitimately forgivable by their victims? Under what circumstances, if any, may perpetrators of such evils ever legitimately forgive themselves? We have all heard the phrase "unforgivable injuries." Are there really unforgivable injuries and, if so, does this make those responsible for such injuries unforgivable also? Have such persons—those responsible for the torture and rape of children, for example—turned themselves into excrement, morally lost and beyond all hope? And is there an important difference between a secular and a religious way of thinking about such questions?

Having briefly sketched the kinds of evils that might seem to pose the greatest obstacles to forgiveness, let me now consider the nature of forgiveness itself.

What is forgiveness? One of the most insightful discussions of forgiveness ever penned is to be found in Bishop Joseph Butler's 1726 sermon "On Forgiveness of Injuries"—a long and closely reasoned philosophical essay that must have greatly tried the patience of his congregation. In that sermon, Butler offers a characterization of forgiveness that I have adapted in my own work on the topic.

According to Butler, forgiveness is a moral virtue (a virtue of character) that is essentially a matter of the heart, the inner self, and involves a change in inner feeling more than a change in external action. The change in feeling is this: the overcoming, on moral grounds, of the intense negative reactive attitudes that are quite naturally occasioned when one has been wronged by another—mainly the vindictive passions of resentment, anger, hatred, and the desire for revenge. A person who has forgiven has overcome those vindictive attitudes and has overcome them for a morally creditable motive—for example, being moved by repentance on the part of the person by whom one has been wronged. Of course, such a change in feeling often leads to a change of behavior—reconciliation, for example; but, as our ability to forgive the dead illustrates, it does not always do so.

On this analysis of forgiveness, it is useful initially to distinguish forgiveness from other responses to wrongdoing with which forgiveness is often confused: justification, excuse, mercy, and reconciliation. Although these concepts are to some degree open textured and can bleed into each other, clarity is—I think—served if one at least starts by attempting to separate them. I will discuss each of them briefly.

1. *Justification*. To regard conduct as justified (as in lawful self-defense, for example) is to claim that the conduct, though normally wrongful, was—in the given circumstances and all things considered—the right thing to do. If I have suffered because of conduct that was right—for example, had my nose bloodied by someone defending himself against my wrongful attack—I have not been wronged, have nothing legitimately to resent, and thus have nothing to forgive.

2. *Excuse*. To regard conduct as excused (as in the insanity defense, for example) is to admit that the conduct was wrong but to claim that the person who engaged in the conduct lacked substantial capacity to conform his conduct to the relevant norms and thus was not a fully responsible agent. Responsible agency is, of course, a matter of degree; but to the degree that the person who injures me is not a responsible agent, resentment of that person would make no more sense than resenting a sudden storm that soaks me. Again, there is nothing here to forgive.

3. *Mercy*. The concepts of mercy and forgiveness are closely related—in part because they both often flow from compassion—but clarity is promoted if they are distinguished. To accord a wrongdoer mercy is to inflict a less harsh consequence on that person than is allowed by institutional (usually legal) rules. Mercy is less personal than

forgiveness, since the one granting mercy (a sentencing judge, say) typically will not be a victim of wrongdoing and thus will not have any feelings of resentment to overcome. (There is a sense in which only victims of wrongdoing have what might be called *standing* to forgive.) Mercy also has a public behavioral dimension not necessarily present in forgiveness. I can forgive a person simply in my heart of hearts, but I cannot show mercy simply in my heart of hearts. I can forgive the dead, but I cannot show mercy to the dead.

This distinction between mercy and forgiveness allows us to see why there is no inconsistency in fully forgiving a person for wrongdoing but still advocating that the person suffer the legal consequence of criminal punishment. To the degree that criminal punishment is justified in order to secure victim satisfaction, then—of course—the fact that the victim has forgiven will be a relevant argument for reducing the criminal's sentence and the fact that a victim still resents and hates will be a relevant argument for increasing that sentence. It is highly controversial, of course, that criminal punishment should to *any* degree be harnessed to victim desires—an issue to be discussed in a later chapter. Even if it is, however, it must surely be admitted that the practice serves other values as well—particularly crime control and justice; and, with respect to these goals, victim forgiveness could hardly be dispositive. In short: It would indeed be inconsistent for a person to claim that he has forgiven the wrongdoer and still advocate punishment for the wrongdoer in order to satisfy his personal vindictive feelings. (If he still has those feelings, he has not forgiven.) It would not be inconsistent, however, to advocate punishment for other legitimate reasons. Of course, the possibilities for self-deception are enormous here. As Nietzsche reminded us, our high-sounding talk about justice and public order is often simply a rationalization for envy, spite, malice, and outright cruelty—the cluster of emotions for which he used the French term *ressentiment*.

4. *Reconciliation.* The vindictive passions (those overcome in forgiveness) are often a major barrier to reconciliation; and thus, since forgiveness often leads to reconciliation, it is easy to confuse the two concepts. I think, however, that it is important also to see how they may differ—how there can be forgiveness without reconciliation and reconciliation without forgiveness.

First let me give an example of forgiveness without reconciliation. Imagine a battered woman who has been repeatedly beaten and raped by her husband or boyfriend. This woman—after a religious conversion, perhaps—might well come to forgive her batterer (i.e., stop hating him) without a willingness to resume her relationship with him. "I forgive you and wish you well" can, in my view, sit quite consistently with "I never want you in this house again." In short, the fact that one has forgiven does not mean that one must also trust or live again with a person.

As an example of reconciliation without forgiveness, consider the example of the South African Truth and Reconciliation Commission. (Note that it is not called the Truth and Forgiveness Commission.) In order to negotiate a viable transition from apartheid to democratic government with full black participation, all parties had to agree that there would in most cases be no punishment for evil acts that occurred under the previous government. Politically motivated wrongdoers, by making a full confession and accepting responsibility, would typically be granted amnesty. In this process the wrongdoers would not be required to repent, show remorse, or even apologize.

I can clearly see this process as one of reconciliation—a process that will (one hopes) allow all to work toward a democratic and just future. I do not so easily see this process as one of forgiveness, however. No change of heart was required or even sought from the victims—no overcoming of such vindictive feelings as resentment and hatred. All that was hoped of them was a willingness to accept this process as a necessary means to the future good of their society.

In my view, this counts as forgiveness only if one embraces what is (to me) a less morally rich definition of forgiveness: forgiveness merely as the waiving of a right. Examples of this are found in the private law idea of forgiving a debt or in Bishop Desmond Tutu's definition of forgiveness as "waiving one's right to revenge." But surely one can waive one's rights for purely instrumental reasons—reasons having nothing to do with the change of heart that constitutes forgiveness as a moral virtue. One can even waive one's rights for selfish reasons—for example, the belief that one's future employment prospects will be better if one simply lets bygones be bygones.

I am not saying, of course, that it is wrong to act for instrumental reasons—indeed, for South Africa, it was probably the only rational course. Neither am I saying that instrumental justifications can never be moral justifications. To attempt reconciliation for the future good of one's society, for example, is surely both instrumental and moral. I am simply saying that, however justified acting instrumentally may sometimes be, it is—absent the extinction of resentment and other vindictive passions—something other than what I understand as the moral virtue of forgiveness. In short: If all we know is that two parties have decided to reconcile, we do not know enough to make a reliable judgment about whether the moral virtue of forgiveness has been realized in the reconciliation.

I propose, then, to understand forgiveness as the overcoming, on moral grounds, of what I will call the *vindictive passions*—the passions of anger, resentment, and even hatred that are often occasioned when one has been deeply wronged by another. These are the passions that often prompt acts of vengeance or revenge, but one can have the passions without acting on them—just as one can feel sexual lust without acting on it.

To what degree is forgiveness, so understood, a good thing? Some would argue that it is obviously a good thing, since the vindictive passions overcome are (like such passions as malicious cruelty and racial hatred) obviously totally bad things.

I think that this totally negative view of the vindictive passions is mistaken—that, contrary to much unjustified bad press they have received, they may play a morally valuable role in human psychology and human relations. And so, in the next chapter, I will lead a couple of cheers for vindictiveness, arguing that some important values may be compromised if one overcomes vindictiveness in hasty forgiveness.

TWO CHEERS FOR VINDICTIVENESS

Vengeance is the infliction of suffering on a person in order to satisfy vindictive emotions or passions. Vindictive emotions are harsh negative passions—anger, resentment, even hatred—often felt by victims toward those who have wronged them. After Agamemnon wrongfully takes his war prize, the girl Briseis, from Achilles, Achilles presents a good example of vindictiveness:

> Not if his gifts outnumbered the sea sands
> or all the dust grains in the world could Agamemnon
> ever appease me—not till he pays me back
> full measure, pain for pain, dishonor for dishonor.
>
> *(Iliad* 9.383–386)

When harm (including legal punishment) is inflicted as vengeance, it may accidentally serve deterrence or retributive purposes. These are not its goals, however. The goal of vengeance is simply to provide vindictive satisfaction to victims, and victims may require for their satisfaction something other than what is necessary to control crime or what wrongdoers deserve.

In the next chapter, I will explore the question of the degree to which, if at all, the satisfaction of victim vindictiveness (or victim forgiveness, for that matter) is a legitimate purpose of criminal punishment.

In this chapter, however, I want to discuss the rationality and moral legitimacy of the passion of vindictiveness itself. If the passion itself is inherently irrational or immoral, then surely it should play *no role whatsoever* in legal punishment—and the next chapter will not be necessary. Who, for example, would want to read a chapter exploring the degree to which racial hatred should play a role in legal punishment? Since that passion is widely regarded as a paradigm of an evil passion, it would be regarded as obvious to almost everybody that it should play no role whatsoever in the law—that wherever it does in fact play a role is an injustice crying out for correction.

However, since I do not regard vindictiveness as inherently irrational or immoral, I will not be able to take the easy route of claiming that it should be kept out of the law simply because of what it is. Its possible legal use will require a separate and careful discussion—one I will attempt to provide in chapter 3.

In this chapter I will for the most part put legal issues to one side and make this question—a question of personal virtue—my central focus: In which category does vindictiveness belong—among those passions that no morally decent person would willingly retain (malice, cruelty, spite, racial hatred, etc.) or among those passions that bring moral credit to the person who possesses them (kindness, generosity, indignation over wrongs done to others, etc.)? Or does it perhaps straddle both of these categories?

I will argue that vindictiveness is somewhat analogous to jealousy with respect to its classification: Since it often provokes wrongful destructive conduct, it is tempting to locate it among the evil passions; however, this temptation can to a substantial degree be overcome when we fully understand the passion and the values to which it is tied. Jerome Neu and others have argued that jealousy is tied to love and, since love is a good thing, jealousy is a good thing to the degree that it is (within rational limits) so tied. I will argue that at least some vindictive passions (particularly resentment) are tied to self-respect and self-defense and, since self-respect and self-defense are good things, a reasonable degree of resentment is a good thing to the degree that it is so tied.

In making a case for at least some of the vindictive passions, let me return again to Bishop Butler. In addition to his powerful sermon on forgiveness, Bishop Butler authored an equally powerful sermon with the title "Upon Resentment." In that sermon, Butler started to make a case for the legitimacy of resentment and other vindictive passions—arguing that a just and loving God would not have universally implanted these passions within his creatures unless the passions served some valuable purpose. (A similar point—without any reference to God—might well be made by an evolutionary biologist.) The danger of resentment, Butler argued, lies not in having it, but rather in being dominated and consumed by it to such a degree that one can never overcome it and acts irresponsibly on the basis of it. As the initial response to being wronged, however, the passion stands in defense of important values—values that might be compromised by immediate and uncritical forgiveness of wrongs.

What are the values defended by resentment and threatened by hasty and uncritical forgiveness? I would suggest three: self-respect, self-defense, and respect for the moral order. A person who never resented any injuries done to him might be a saint. It is equally likely, however, that his lack of resentment reveals a servile personality—a personality lacking in respect for himself and respect for his rights and status as a free and equal moral being. (This is the point behind the S. J. Perelman quip previously quoted: "To err is human; to forgive, supine.") Just as indignation or guilt over the mistreatment of others stands as emotional testimony that we care about them and their rights, so does resentment stand as emotional testimony that we care about ourselves and our rights.

This is a very important point to emphasize: Moral commitment is not merely a matter of intellectual allegiance; it requires emotional allegiance as well, for a moral person is not simply a person who holds the abstract belief that certain things are wrong. The moral person is also *motivated* to do something about the wrong—and the source of our motivation lies primarily in our passions or emotions.

Intellectually believing something and actually feeling it in your guts emotionally are, of course, two quite distinct things—although we like to deceive ourselves into confusing them. The philosopher Peter Geach tells the story of an Anglican archdeacon who was asked what he expected after death. The archdeacon replied: "I expect to enjoy eternal bliss at the feet of my God, but please let us stop talking about such depressing matters."

So, in short, the virtuous person will not simply say and believe in a purely intellectual way that he respects himself as a free and equal moral being with basic rights; he will also react emotionally if he is not treated as such a being. What Peter Strawson calls the "reactive attitude" of resentment, directed toward wrongs and those who do the wrongs, is a paradigm example of such emotional response.

Related to all this is an instrumental point: Those who have vindictive dispositions toward those who wrong them give potential wrongdoers an incentive *not* to wrong them. If I were going to set out to oppress other people, I would surely prefer to select for my victims persons whose first response is forgiveness rather than persons whose first response is revenge. As Kant noted, "One who makes himself into a worm cannot complain if people step on him."

It is important to stress, however, that resentment does not stand simply as emotional testimony of self-respect. This passion—and the reluctance to transcend it in hasty forgiveness—also stands as testimony to our allegiance to the moral order itself. We all have a duty to support—both intellectually and emotionally—the moral order, an order represented by clear understandings of what constitutes unacceptable treatment of one human being by another. If we do not show some resentment to those who, in victimizing us, flout those understandings, then we run the risk—in Aurel Kolnai's words—of being "complicitous in evil."

A balanced view of the vindictive passions—one both appreciating their value and recognizing their dangers—can sometimes be found in ancient Greek philosophy and literature. Indeed, one of the earliest justifications for legal punishment and the rule of law is presented by the character of Athena in the final play of Aeschylus's *Oresteia* trilogy. The vindictive passions, she reasons, are not in themselves either irrational or evil. They represent, indeed, legitimate emotional indicators of self-respect, self-defense, and allegiance to the moral and social order. Thus the Furies—who represent these passions—will not be banished from Athens but will rather be given an honorable home there.

Their honorable home, however, will come with a certain price tag: the costs and burdens of *institutionalization*. No longer will individual victims of wrongdoing be free to pursue individual—and thus unpredictable and socially dangerous—revenge. Rather the community will, as it were, take on the *personae* of victims and act in their names—act in the regular, procedural, proportional, and predictable manner that we associate with the rule of law. Thus will the Furies be transformed into the Eumenides, or "Kindly Ones." No longer expressive merely of unfettered private revenge-seeking, they will represent not vigilante activity (with which revenge should not be confused) but the pursuit of revenge under the constraints of law. Victim satisfaction—including the satisfaction of vindictive passions—will be an aim of law, but it will by no means be the sole aim, for it will be limited by the aim of due process.

Athena's way of dealing with the vindictive passions did not, of course, survive unchallenged into the present day. With the arrival of Stoicism—and particularly with the arrival of Christianity—we see an attack on the legitimacy of the vindictive passions themselves, and not merely on their expression in private vigilante activities. In these traditions, the passion for revenge or getting even is often (but not always) seen as intrinsically irrational or evil or both.

Two important questions arise at this point: First, is the modern opposition to vindictiveness deeply felt, or is it something to which mainly public lip service is paid? Second, is the opposition to vindictiveness really plausible, given what I have—following Bishop Butler—been able to say on its behalf?

In considering the first question, it must be acknowledged that opposition to vindictiveness has taken firm roots in ordinary language, for merely to call a person "vindictive" is normally taken to express serious criticism of that person. What we say is not always a perfect reflection of what we really believe and how we really feel, however—recall the story of the archdeacon—and thus my hunch is that general support for the vindictive passions is greater than one might initially suppose.

Consider, for example, the great popularity of revenge entertainment—for example, films such as the western *Silverado.* in which decent people, long victimized by thugs of unspeakable brutality, finally strike back and take their justified revenge on those who have wronged them. Such films are extremely popular, and my bet is that most people (including those who regard themselves as decent and enlightened) take considerable private vicarious delight in seeing revenge portrayed. And who does not resonate with *some* sympathy to the sentiments expressed by the late *Chicago Tribune* columnist Mike Royko when he covered the execution of Steven Judy? Royko wrote:

> The small crowd that gathered outside the prison to protest the execution of Steven Judy softly sang "We Shall Overcome." . . . But it didn't seem quite the same hearing it sung out of concern for someone who, on finding a woman with a flat tire, raped and murdered her and drowned her three small children, then said that he hadn't been "losing any sleep" over his crimes. (quoted in Moore, 1987, p. 184)

I tend to side with those theorists of knowledge who suggest that we operate with a bias in favor of common sense—imposing the burden of proof on those who would challenge our shared common-sense beliefs. If I am correct in my assumption that beliefs in the appropriateness of revenge are among our common-sense beliefs (in spite of what we feel obliged to say), and if I am correct in thinking that Butler has given us at least some reason to consider sympathetically the vindictive passions, then it may be reasonable to impose—for a change—the burden of proof on those who would challenge beliefs in their legitimacy—impose on them the burden of actually *arguing* for the irrationality or immorality of these emotions, and not merely trotting out sentimental clichés.

Now I know that some people will find it odd to claim that emotions can be evaluated as either rational or irrational. Are not emotions, they will ask, something totally different from reason—arational—and thus beyond all rational evaluation? In asking if an emotion is rational or irrational, is this not like asking the silly question if a headache is rational or irrational?

This way of thinking is clearly mistaken and tends to rest on a confusion between emotions and sensations. With respect to sensations—headaches, tickles, orgasms—it is indeed senseless to inquire into their rationality. But emotions are more complex, since they involve a component—belief—that is open to rational evaluation. There is no belief that is an intrinsic part of my having a headache, but the emotion of guilt (for example) cannot be understood or distinguished from other emotions except in terms of the constitutive belief that one has done something wrong. And were there is belief there is the possibility of irrational belief.

So how might one argue that the emotion of vindictiveness is irrational? I think that the arguments fall into two camps: (1) arguments seeking to show that the vindictive passions are themselves irrational or immoral or both, or (2) arguments seeking to show that these passions, whatever their intrinsic merits (which may be considerable), have no legitimate place within the law or other social institutions.

Since I will explore the second argument in the next chapter, I will close this chapter by examining the first argument—the argument that the vindictive passions are themselves without positive value, irrational or immoral or both.

One normally argues for the irrationality of an emotion by attempting to show that it is not fitting to its object, is harmful to the person who experiences the emotion, is inherently self-defeating, necessarily leads to pathological and dangerous excess (also an argument for its immorality), or is pointless—lacking in any useful purpose.

I do not think that vindictiveness can easily be shown to be irrational on any of these tests. It certainly *seems* fitting that one strikes back when one has been injured—indeed, such a response seems encoded in us by our evolutionary history—and thus the vindictive person does not seem like the neurotic who does indeed have an emotion that is not fitting to its object—for example, a person who is *phobic*, who has an irrational fear of objects that are not in fact dangerous. Neither does the emotion seem pointless. Vindictive people want to get even and no doubt will often, having asserted their own equal worth and rights, feel much better when such revenge is realized. That just is its point. To say it is pointless only because it does not have a point of which the critic of vindictiveness would approve is simply to beg the question at issue.

Nietzsche famously argued that the vindictive person tends to harm himself—like a scorpion stinging itself to death with its own tail. It is, of course, irrational to regard as legitimate an emotion that is self-poisoning, and this looks like a good case for the irrationality of vindictiveness. But such a conclusion would, I think, be hasty for two reasons.

First, what Nietzsche really argues is that vindictiveness (what he calls *ressentiment*) will poison if *repressed*; and this is as much an argument in favor of expressing our vindictiveness in acts of revenge as it is an argument for the elimination of vindictiveness.

Second, we need to distinguish between the rationality of an emotion itself and the rationality of the *role* that this emotion plays in the life of a person. Recall Spinoza on the fear of death. He did not argue that the fear itself is irrational. He did not, for example, counsel against looking both ways before crossing a street. Rather he argued that it is irrational to be *led* by the fear of death—to let the fear play such a dominant role in one's life that it sours all the good things that life has to offer. Thus, unless it can be shown that vindictiveness must always be the dominant passion and thus lead the vindictive person in some self-destructive or other-destructive way, we do not yet have a case for the irrationality of the passion itself.

Of course, some writers have argued this very thing—have argued that vindictiveness will in fact always so dominate a person's life as to prevent that person's human flourishing. Listen, for example, to the psychoanalyst Karen Horney on vindictiveness. She writes:

> There is no more holding back a person driven toward revenge than an alcoholic determined to go on a binge. Any reasoning meets with cold disdain. Logic no longer prevails. Whether or not the situation is appropriate does not matter. It overrides prudence. Consequences for himself and others are brushed aside. He is as inaccessible as anybody who is in the grip of a blind passion. (Horney, 1948, p. 5)

This is a serious claim, since—if true—it would reveal the vindictive person as having not only an irrational self but also an immoral self—a self likely to harm others and to undermine social order.

But is Horney's claim true? I have my doubts. Speaking (as almost any Irishman can) from extensive personal experience as a rather vindictive person, I believe that I have often gotten even with people by actions that were moderate and proportional—perhaps involving nothing more than a few well selected (and hopefully hurtful) words or by actions no more extreme than no longer extending lunch invitations or rides to work to them.

And rarely have I been dominated by my vindictive feelings. I often let them float harmlessly in the back of my mind until an appropriate occasion for their expression occurs. I am not suggesting that this makes me particularly admirable—only that it hardly qualifies me as crazy or evil.

Where then do we get this idea that vindictive people are dangerously crazy and destructive? I think that we get it primarily from art—particularly film and literature, where revenge is often mistakenly identified with illegal and socially disruptive vigilante activity that at least borders on insanity.

A good example of this is the story of Michael Kohlhaas in the novella *Michael Kohlhaas by* Heinrich von Kleist—a story retold by E. L. Doctorow in his novel *Ragtime*, where Michael Kohlhaas becomes Coalhouse Walker. This story illustrates the kind of crazy excess to which vindictive people can be driven: Kohlhaas, a benevolent horse dealer, has his animals mistreated by an aristocratic neighbor when he cannot pay the illegal toll newly required by the aristocrat for crossing his land. When the law (administered by friends of the aristocrat) will not provide him the just compensation he seeks, he starts on a campaign of vengeful murder that ultimately destroys his business, leads to the death of his wife, and starts a revolution so threatening to the integrity of the state that Martin Luther must intervene to try and stop him. A great story, indeed—as is its retelling in *Ragtime*.

But what does the story show? That vindictiveness is inherently crazy or simply that sometimes—as can happen with *any* passion—some vindictive people act in pathological ways and let their passions get out of hand? The story would have been *boring* had Kohlhaas taken his revenge in more moderate ways (burning the toll booth or even thrashing the aristocrat, perhaps) but this does not demonstrate that moderate and proportional revenge taking is not possible. Nuttiness is simply more dramatic and interesting than just proportionality. However, we must not assume that because the pathological cases are more interesting that there are not plenty of non-pathological cases. Art sometimes trumps psychological accuracy.

Finally, is a strategy of revenge inherently self-defeating? Jean Hampton (in our jointly authored book *Forgiveness and Mercy*) argued that it is. According to Hampton, we feel lowered by people who wrong us and are tempted to hurt them in order to drop them from their superior position—an act of revenge that allows us now to feel superior to them. (The idea of overcoming a perceived inequality is surely the dominant idea behind the metaphor of "getting even.") But if we succeed in hurting them—Hampton argues—our revenge is hollow; for who can take satisfaction in harming a lowered being?

This argument is clever, but I do not think it works. Perhaps the most it shows is that satisfying revenge does not always require as much harm to the wrongdoer as one might initially have thought. Just getting the person in a position where one has the *power* to inflict harm may be satisfying enough, and that may itself be the revenge. Franny, in John Irving's novel *The Hotel New Hampshire*, seeks revenge against the man who led the gang that raped her. In a scene that is both very terrifying and very funny, she arranges to have him sodomized by one of her friends dressed up in a costume that makes the friend appear to be a very wild and very horny bear. At the last minute, however, Franny's inherent decency is moved by the pitiful crying and begging person she sees groveling before the "bear," and she lets the rapist crawl away unraped. This does not show, however, that she did not get revenge. Rather it shows that adequate revenge was found simply in having the power to rape the person who had raped her. Going through with the actual rape was not necessary.

My conclusion: None of the arguments I have surveyed establishes either the irrationality or immorality of vindictiveness.

Since the arguments against vindictiveness are weak, and since something has been found to say in its favor, I think that it is justified to conclude—at least provisionally—that vindictive passions can legitimately be attributed to sane and virtuous people. Virtuous people can, I think, sometimes even enjoy without guilt the knowledge that those who have wronged them are "getting theirs."

It does not follow from this, however, that sane and virtuous people always act rightly in acting out these passions—in actually being instrumental in seeing that others "get theirs." Neither does it follow that the law ought to be a vehicle for such acting out. Feeling vindictive is one thing, but actually seeking vengeance or getting even—personally or through the law—is quite a different thing, and that will be the subject of the next chapter.

Before beginning that chapter, however, let me address a question that may have arisen in the minds of some of my readers. Given that I have had much to say in defense of vindictiveness, and given that I have tried to blunt the standard criticisms of it, why did the title of the present chapter offer only two cheers for vindictiveness? Why not three? The answer to that question will be found in chapter 4, where I begin to explore the virtue of forgiveness.

THREE

VINDICTIVENESS AND THE LAW

Does vindictiveness have a place in the law? Even if vindictiveness is not inherently irrational, there may still be good reasons for thinking that the passion should be kept out of the law. Kant argued this way about compassion. This emotion, though admirable and properly expressed in many contexts, would—in his view—tend to undermine justice if allowed to enter into criminal sentencing.

In order to consider possible reasons for opposing vindictiveness in the law, it might be useful to look at an area of law that currently seems to allow vindictiveness a limited role: the use of *victim impact statements* in criminal sentencing. (Similar testimony may also be sought in parole, clemency, and pardon hearings.)

Victim impact statements are statements presented by crime victims (or by surviving family members in murder cases) whose purpose is to influence those with discretionary sentencing authority. Although these statements are sometimes religiously based pleas for forgiveness and mercy, they are most often angry (and presumably vindictive) demands that the sentencing authority impose the harshest possible sentence.

One reason that has been given in support of the use of victim impact statements in sentencing is that the statements may be highly therapeutic for the victims or survivors—allowing them to vent their anger, feel that they have played some important role in what happens to the person who has victimized them, and achieve what is now—I am growing tired of the phrase—generally called "closure."

Although the empirical evidence here is probably mixed, suppose for a moment that victim impact statements might reasonably be believed to perform various valuable functions for victims. Is there any reason why one among the many purposes of criminal sentencing should not be the satisfaction of such victim desires—particularly if a majority of citizens (through their representatives) manifest a preference for such a purpose? What is a democracy, after all, if not a form of government that allows the collective will to determine policy in such matters?

The short and quick answer to this question, of course, is that contemporary democracies are not pure democracies but are rather constitutionally constrained democracies. There are some things the majority may not do, some preferences they may not get to satisfy, if there are important reasons of principle that would be compromised by their satisfaction. With respect to punishment, such principles are found in the ban in the United States Constitution's Eighth Amendment on "cruel and unusual punishments" and in the Fourteenth Amendment requirements of due process and equal protection.

Do victim impact statements run afoul of these principles? Justice Lewis Powell, writing for the majority in the 1987 case of *Booth v. Maryland,* argued that they do. Powell feared that, by introducing such powerful emotions into criminal sentencing, arbitrary and capricious sentencing will result. The criminal's sentence may depend not on what is truly relevant to criminal liability—personal desert and responsibility—but rather on whether the criminal's victim is attractive, articulate, and persuasive. This, argued Powell, is a matter of luck rather than desert; and any sentencing practice resting on luck rather than desert should be declared unconstitutional.

Justices Antonin Scalia and Byron White, in their dissents in *Booth,* were highly critical of Justice Powell's reasoning. Criminal sentencing is already shot through with luck, they argued, and so it is rather late in the day to be claiming that our system of criminal liability is based solely on personal responsibility and desert. Consider, for example, the differential punishments for murder and attempted murder. Sometimes this difference rests totally on luck, as when an attempt to murder fails through a fortuity—for example, the gun misfires. Any system that apportions punishment to harm will, they argue, sometimes be basing sentencing on luck. And if a person may be punished more severely because he had the bad luck to have a gun that worked, or a victim whose blood would not clot, what is wrong with punishing more severely a criminal who had the bad luck to kill someone with attractive and articulate relatives who care?

On an unsympathetic interpretation of the Scalia and White argument—one that their texts sometimes invite—they seem to be suggesting that, since the system already has a few arbitrary and capricious (and thus arguably unjust) elements, why not a few more? This reasoning would, of course, be morally unacceptable. On a more charitable interpretation, however, Scalia and White have raised an interesting and difficult point. I think that they make some mistakes in what they argue, but the mistakes are neither simple nor simple-minded. The relation between luck, harm, and justified punishment is complex.

We do, as they noted, punish successful murder much more severely than attempted murder; and success or failure here often depends on luck (e.g., on whether the gun fired properly). Is this just or at least justified?

Common sense and common practice seem to answer yes, and, since I have already expressed an inclination to pay some deference to common sense, I cannot simply dismiss this. I can, however, say this: Many of my students, who are inclined to be retributivists and believe that punishment ought to be proportional to personal desert and responsibility, often—after a discussion of attempt cases—move rather quickly away from the common view with which they started to the view that, contrary to present practice, attempted murder that fails through a fortuity perhaps should *not* be punished less severely than successful murder. So common sense (at least common retributive sense) may be rather fluid on this issue.

However, even those students who are willing to accommodate luck and hold on to their original common-sense belief that the punishment for attempts should be less severe than the punishment for successes do not generally want the criminal to endure harsher consequences because of the bad luck of having an attractive, articulate, and persuasive victim. Common sense seems to suggest that not all instances of luck should be treated equally and that this luck is irrelevant, whatever one's view about the relevance of other instances of luck may be.

Perhaps these students are grasping here that one of the purposes of the criminal law is the nonretributive purpose of preventing wrongful harm—thus the legitimacy of the command "Do not risk wrongfully hurting people." This command is clearly violated in unsuccessful attempts that fail through a fortuity.

Giving special protection to those who are articulate and attractive, however, is not one of the acceptable purposes of the criminal law—thus the obvious illegitimacy of the command "Take special care not to risk wrongfully harming those who are attractive, articulate, and persuasive." The former command enshrines values we openly embrace; the latter command does not.

A second and related argument against victim impact statements used by Powell (an argument growing out of the foregoing and one that I find very persuasive) is also in my view inadequately addressed by the dissent—namely, that victim impact statements have a tendency to move us away from our egalitarian commitments to the principle that all crime victims are created equal. There is a danger that middle-class, presentable, and articulate victims will make their losses seem more important—and thus more worthy of harsh punishment—than the losses experienced by crime victims who are social outsiders.

The importance of this point was generally lost in the dissents written by Scalia and White. When the composition of the court changed, however, Scalia and White had more supporters for their dissent; and thus *Booth* was overruled in 1991 in *Payne v. Tennessee.*

In short: Although I am, for all the reasons previously given, reluctant to present a blanket condemnation of the vindictive passions and those who express them, I see danger in allowing these passions to find legal expression in victim impact statements.

Justices Scalia and White have still raised one very important point, however, and I would not want to see it lost. As they note, our present system of criminal law often makes severity of punishment a function of the *harm* actually caused—punishing, for example, murder far more severely than attempted murder that fails through a fortuity. However, if actual harm caused is often a matter of luck (e.g., a misfiring gun) then actual harm caused is neither an accurate indicator of the badness of the person nor an accurate indicator of the dangerousness of that person. In such cases neither a retributive justification for lesser punishment (punishment in proportion to moral desert) nor a crime control justification for lesser punishment (punish in proportion to dangerousness) is applicable.

Why then do we punish more severely in the one case than in the other? I suspect that the answer may lie in vengeance or revenge—the idea that when harm occurs it is necessary to pay back, to get even, for what was done quite independently of considerations of desert or social utility.

To the degree that considerations of payback or getting even are at work, then the legal satisfaction of the vindictive passions may not be confined merely to the arena of victim impact statements but may be present in the criminal law as a whole. Do we want to overhaul the criminal law so as to make harm irrelevant? Or should we instead keep the law as it is and openly acknowledge that its present structure contains at least an element of vengeance? And might not victims or survivors provide relevant—if not decisive—evidence on the degree of harm caused? I leave these questions for the reader to ponder.

Where has the discussion reached to this point? I have tried so far to make the best case I can for vindictiveness and revenge-taking. I have been motivated to do this because I fear that the case against vindictiveness has often been driven more by slogans than by persuasive argument.

I fear also that those who unambiguously condemn vindictiveness sometimes reveal a class bias that is unseemly in a society that claims to be committed to a principle of equal concern and respect for all citizens. Vindictiveness is often condemned by the educated, the privileged, and the sheltered—something they regard as found mainly among those regarded as uneducated rednecks and other assorted trailer trash. I, however, do not want to go down this road. If a substantial number of my fellow citizens are strongly committed to some belief or some passion, I do not want simply to assume—because it is not a passion or belief normally celebrated in my social circle—that there is nothing to be said for it.

I want instead to portray vindictiveness as complex—a mixture of good and bad elements—and thereby avoid the simplistic reductionism often found in those who condemn this passion. So I have tried to say something for vindictiveness and revenge—enough, I hope, at least to constitute the two cheers I promised.

In discussing the *Booth* case, however, I started to express a bit of support for those who oppose vindictiveness—at least in its more dramatic public and legal manifestations. I now want to continue in this vein and explore the idea that, even if vindictiveness is neither inherently irrational nor inherently immoral, it does pose some particularly dramatic dangers that should impose severe cautions on our willingness to be led—or approve of others being led—by this passion.

It is time to consider the virtue of forgiveness.

FOUR

FORGIVENESS AS A VIRTUE

It is, of course, possible, as I have argued already, to take one's revenge against others in measured and proportional and peaceful ways—ways as simple as a cutting remark before colleagues or a failure to continue issuing lunch invitations. But even these modest acts of revenge can seem petty and hardly to one's credit, since they may reveal a kind of tit-for-tat scorekeeping mentality, making it likely that one is developing what Nietzsche called the soul of an accountant or shopkeeper.

A much more serious danger arises, of course, when victimized people or those who sympathize with them allow vindictiveness to take over their very selves—turning them into self-righteous fanatics so involved, even joyous, in their outrage that they will be satisfied only with the utter cruel annihilation of the wrongdoer. Recall, in this regard, the revolting "Ted Bundy Memorial Barbecue" that was staged outside the prison where Bundy was being electrocuted.

Karen Horney certainly overstated the case in thinking that vindictive people are *always* like that, but she was on to something important: vindictive people are *often* like that. Such people are sometimes even willing to destroy, as symbolic stand-ins, persons who have done them no wrong or who may even be totally innocent. (*Michael Kohlhaas,* the novella by von Kleist that I have already mentioned, is a famous illustration of this.) Such persons pose a threat to the morality and decency of the social order—particularly when they, perhaps unconsciously, use the language of justice and crime control as a rationalization for what is really sadism and cruelty. And I fear that the potential to be such a person is latent in all of us. I cannot help thinking, for example, that many of the unspeakably brutish conditions that we tolerate in our jails and prisons flow not from stated legitimate desires for justice and crime control but rather from a vindictiveness so out of control that it actually becomes a kind of malice. If we are tempted so to demonize those who have wronged us and start viewing them as monsters, we would be wise to recall Nietzsche's famous warning: "Take care that when you do battle with monsters that you do not become a monster."

Against such a background, forgiveness can be seen as a healing virtue that brings with it great blessings—chief among them being its capacity to free us from being consumed by our angers, its capacity to check our tendencies toward cruelty, and its capacity (in some cases) to open the door to the restoration of those relationships in our lives that are worthy of restoration. This last blessing can be seen in the fact that, since all of us will sometimes wrong the people who mean the most to us, there will be times when we will want to be forgiven by those whom we have wronged. Seeing this, no rational person would desire to live in a world where forgiveness was not seen as a healing virtue. This is, I take it, the secular insight in the parable of the unforgiving servant at Matthew 18:21–35, which I will give myself the pleasure of quoting in the King James version:

> Therefore is the kingdom of heaven likened unto a certain king, which would take account of his servants. And when he had begun to reckon, one was brought unto him which owed him ten thousand talents. But foreasmuch as he had not to pay, his lord commanded him to be sold, and his wife, and children, and all that he had, and payment to be made. The servant therefore fell down and worshipped him, saying, Lord, have patience with me, and I will pay thee all. Then the lord of that servant was moved with compassion, and loosed him, and forgave him the debt. But the same servant when out, and found one of his fellow-servants, which owed him an hundred pence: and he laid hands on him, and took him by the throat, saying, Pay me that thou owest. And his fellow-servant fell down at his feet, and besought him, saying, Have patience with me, and I will pay thee all. And he would not: but went and cast him into prison, till he should pay the debt. . . .Then his lord, after that he had called him, said unto him, O thou wicked servant, I forgave thee all that debt, because thou desiredst me: Shouldest not thou also have had compassion on thy fellow-servant, even as I had pity on thee? And his lord was

wroth, and delivered him to the tormentors. . . . So likewise shall
my heavenly Father do also unto you, if ye from your hearts forgive not everyone his brother their trespasses.

We are faced, then, with a complex dilemma: How are we to reap
the blessings of forgiveness without sacrificing our self-respect or our
respect for the moral order in the process—a respect that is often
evinced in resentment and other vindictive passions?

One great help here—and I make no claim that it is the only help
or even a necessary condition for forgiveness—is sincere *repentance* on
the part of the wrongdoer. When I am wronged by another, a great
part of the injury—over and above any physical harm I may suffer—is
the insulting or degrading message that has been given to me by the
wrongdoer: the message that I am less worthy than he is, so unworthy
that he may use me merely as a means or object in service to his desires
and projects. Thus failing to resent (or hastily forgiving) the wrongdoer runs the risk that I am endorsing that very immoral message for
which the wrongdoer stands. If the wrongdoer sincerely repents,
however, he now joins me in repudiating the degrading and insulting
message—allowing me to relate to him (his new self) as an equal without fear that a failure to resent him will be read as a failure to resent
what he has done. In short: It is much easier to follow St. Augustine's
counsel that we should "hate the sin but not the sinner" when the sinner (the wrongdoer) repudiates his own wrongdoing through an act of
repentance.

Repentance is a subject of sufficient importance and complexity
that I will devote an entire chapter to it later. At this point, however,
perhaps I can say with some confidence this much: It is not unreasonable to want repentance from a wrongdoer before forgiving that wrongdoer, since, in the absence of repentance, hasty forgiveness may harm
both the forgiver and the wrongdoer. The forgiver may be harmed by a
failure to show self-respect. The wrongdoer may be harmed by being
deprived of an important incentive—the desire to be forgiven—that
could move him toward repentance and moral rebirth.

Although I plan to explore the relation between forgiveness and religion (particularly Christianity) later, I want here briefly to address a
worry that at this point may have arisen in the minds of some Christian
readers—readers who believe that Christianity commands unconditional forgiveness.

Does Christianity in fact require forgiveness without condition? I
am hardly qualified to express expert views on such theological matters,

but I will presume at least to caution against hasty leaps based merely on a few scriptural passages in English translation.

Within my own religious community (Anglican), I was recently involved in a discussion of the issue of conditional versus unconditional forgiveness. I have long held the view—expressed here—that forgiveness should generally await repentance. Others, however, vigorously claimed that Christianity teaches universal forgiveness and that making forgiveness contingent on repentance borders on blasphemy—a claim supported by two scriptural passages in English translation: Jesus' words from the cross, "Father forgive them for they know not what they do" and the passage in the Lord's Prayer, "Forgive us our trespasses as we forgive those who trespass against us."

I would not presume to offer a decisive opinion about correct Christian theology on the issue of forgiveness, but I do think that universal and unconditional forgiveness—that is, forgiveness not contingent on repentance—by no means gets clear support from either of the two quoted passages.

Jesus' words from the cross are surely *not* offering universal forgiveness. Indeed, Jesus takes the trouble to offer a *reason* why forgiveness should be bestowed on *these particular wrongdoers*—namely, their ignorance that they are sacrificing the true son of God. (Do you think—in different circumstances—he would have said "Father forgive them even though they know full well what they are doing"?)

And consider the passage from the Lord's Prayer. One natural reading of the English word "as" is "in the manner of"—for example, "Do it as I do." Thus one perfectly natural reading of the passage from the Lord's Prayer passage "forgive us our trespasses as we forgive those who trespass against us" is this: "In the realm of forgiveness, God, I pray that you treat me in the manner that I treat those who wrong me. If I will not forgive them unless they repent, I do not expect you to forgive me unless I repent."

Again, I make this point not as a decisive contribution to the Christian theology of forgiveness. I am simply trying to show that, if one wants to articulate a fully Christian theology of forgiveness, one will need something more than a few scriptural passages in English translation. If one wants to play this quotation game, however, then one should—in fairness—quote also Luke 17:3: "If thy brother trespass against thee, rebuke him; and if he repent, forgive him."

My point so far has been to suggest that it is not unreasonable to make forgiveness contingent on sincere repentance. Such repentance at the very least opens the door to forgiveness and often to reconciliation.

This is not to suggest, however, that we should seek to *coerce* repentance as a condition for forgiveness and reconciliation. When a person comes to repentance as a result of his own spiritual growth, we are witness to an inspiring transformation of character. Any expressed repentance that is nothing more than a response to a coercive external incentive, however, is very likely to be fake. This is one reason why the South Africans were probably wise in not demanding repentance as a condition for amnesty in their Truth and Reconciliation Commission

So let us welcome repentance when we find it, and let us do what we can to create a climate where it can flourish and open the door to the moral rebirth of the wrongdoer and to forgiveness by the wronged. But, out of respect for the genuine article, let us not seek to coerce it. Coercing tends to produce only lying and may even be degrading to the wrongdoer—inviting his further corruption rather than his moral rebirth.

David Lurie, the central character in J. M. Coetzee's recent novel *Disgrace*, could save his job if he simply expressed the kind of repentance demanded of him by the university disciplinary board that has authority over him. I find myself sympathizing with the reasons he gives for not giving them what they want when he says:

> We went through the repentance business yesterday. I told you what I thought. I won't do it. I appeared before an officially constituted tribunal, before a branch of the law. Before that secular tribunal I pleaded guilty, a secular plea. That plea should suffice. Repentance is neither here nor there. Repentance belongs to another world, to another universe of discourse. . . . [What you are asking] reminds me too much of Mao's China. Recantation, self-criticism, public apology. I'm old fashioned, I would prefer simply to be put against a wall and shot. (Coetzee, 1999, p. 58)

There has in recent times been much cheap and shallow chatter about forgiveness and repentance—some of it coming from high political officials and some coming from the kind of psychobabble often found in self-help and recovery books. As a result of this, many people are, I fear, starting to become cynical about both. For reasons I have developed here, repentance may pave the way for forgiveness, which may, in turn, pave the way for reconciliation. It is less likely to do so, however, in a world where we come to believe that too many claims of repentance are insincere and expedient—talking the talk without (so far as we can tell) walking the walk.

I have, with Bishop Butler, tried to stress the virtue of forgiveness while at the same time acknowledging some value in the vindictive passions that forgiveness must often overcome. As long as there is evil in the world—and I would not advise holding one's breath until there is not—we should not, I think, welcome a world free of resentment and other vindictive passions. But neither should we welcome a world dominated by these passions. What we should seek, as Aristotle said with respect to anger, is that these passions be expressed at the right time, in the right way, at the right person, and in consistency with other important values. Given general human depravity and tendencies toward self-deception, however, this is much easier said than done. And so I think we must hope that a cautious and critical commitment to forgiveness—in contrast to a thoughtless and sentimental one—will help us to muddle through, to stumble along as best as is humanly possible in a world where value is fragile and where evil often seems triumphant.

Having laid out a general framework for thinking about the tension between vindictiveness and forgiveness—and the value of both—I would now like to explore in some detail three related specific issues that I have up to this point only mentioned in passing: repentance, self-forgiveness, and forgiveness in psychotherapy.

FIVE

REPENTANCE, PUNISHMENT,
AND MERCY

In the previous chapter, I suggested that sincere (uncoerced) repentance might reasonably be made a condition of forgiveness. I did not analyze the concept of repentance in much detail, however. In this chapter, I will try to offer such an analysis.

I will, of course, explore the moral status of repentance, but I will explore its possible legal status as well—in particular the role it might legitimately play in the granting of mercy. I have already suggested that mercy is a virtue different from forgiveness, but the two virtues relate to each other in interesting ways—for example, a person possessing the virtue of *compassion* is more likely to be both forgiving and merciful.

As we enter the millennium (in at least one sense of that word) the newspapers are filled with talk of repentance. Pope John Paul has suggested that the Catholic Church repent for some of the injustices against non-Catholics to which it has been party during its history; the American Catholic bishops have called for (among other things) repentance from pedophile priests and the bishops who sheltered them; the American Southern Baptist Convention has publicly repented its role in American slavery and racism; and Jacques Chirac, the president of France, has attempted to express, for his country, repentance for its cooperative role in the Nazi extermination of French Jews. The government of Japan has struggled with developing a public response to its atrocities during World War II against other Asian nations—some officials advocating full repentance and others more cautious expressions of sorrow or regret—and the government of Argentina is still struggling with the nature and degree of its public response to the atrocities committed against its own citizens in the "dirty war" during the regime of the generals. America, though taking a qualified public stand of repentance with respect to its wartime internment of Japanese Americans in concentration camps, has so far not taken such a stand with respect to slavery (perhaps at most appropriate for only some states), genocide against Native Americans, or the terror-obliteration bombing of German and Japanese cities during World War II. All of these possible acts of repentance have been advocated, however, by some voices of influence in American politics and opinion.

In sharp contrast to this talk about what might be called *collective* or *group* repentance (and all the logical and moral problems in which such talk is immersed), we rarely hear much talk these days about *individual* repentance. These two facts may, of course, be related, since a stress on collective responsibility could well have a tendency to weaken feelings of individual responsibility. Living (at least in America) in what some have called a "culture of victims," we have seen in recent years the development of various strategies to allow wrongdoers to avoid responsibility for their wrongdoing by claiming victim status for themselves, and a world without responsibility is a world in which repentance lacks logical space.

Gone, it seems, are the days when we could comfortably refer to prisons as *penitentiaries*—places where we would send responsible wrongdoers in order to encourage their repentance. Most people simply do not now value repentance the way it was valued in the past; and the world has, in my view, suffered a loss thereby. Perhaps the concept is now seen as some vestigial relic of a religious worldview to which most people, at most, pay only lip service. Or perhaps, even if the value of repentance is accepted in certain contexts it is not seen as important in a system of criminal law and punishment organized around secular values. It is even possible—given the realities of crime and punishment in America—that it is no longer possible to in honesty see jails and prisons as anything more than fortresses in which are warehoused an alienated underclass that is perceived, often quite accurately, as highly dangerous to the stability of ordinary life.

Given this background, to write on repentance and its relation to criminal punishment may seem to be little more than an exercise in historical nostalgia—an exercise having little relevance to the realities of the world in which we live. One is really in no position to claim this with confidence, however, until the concept of repentance has been explored in the light of contemporary thinking and contemporary realities. Such an exploration is the object of this chapter.

What is repentance? Repentance may be conceptualized as either an interior mental act or as an act with an essential social dimension. As an interior act, it may be seen simply as the remorseful acceptance of responsibility for the evil that one sees in one's character, the repudiation of that evil, and the sincere resolve to do one's best to extirpate it. Montaigne, in his essay "Of Repentance," expressed the interior view when he wrote that "Repentance is nothing but a disavowal of our own will and an opposition to our fancies."

It is easy to see why repentance so conceptualized could be seen as an important moral or religious virtue—for example, as a step toward that "purity of heart" Kierkegaard spoke of—but it is hard to see why the state, particularly the modern secular state, should concern itself with such matters. Indeed, Kierkegaard—in his *Purity of Heart*—saw the state and the social relations over which it presides as a positive *enemy* of repentance in this purely interior sense because it will tempt a person to confuse "the improvement toward society" with what really matters for the sinner: "the resigning of himself to God."

If repentance is to have important consequences for the social community—and for the legal system that partially binds that community together—it will be necessary to develop a concept of repentance that moves beyond the purely inner sphere and into the arena of social relations.

Consider this definition: Repentance is the remorseful acceptance of responsibility for one's wrongful and harmful actions, the repudiation of the aspects of one's character that generated the actions, the resolve to do one's best to extirpate those aspects of one's character, and the resolve to atone or make amends for the harm that one has done. Here the social dimension is obvious—both in the matters over which one is remorseful (wrongful harm to others and not merely a sinful character) and in the final steps of the repentance process (a recognition that one's evil had a *victim*—either a discrete individual or the entire community—and a desire to make that victim whole again).

Even if we grant the social dimension of this sense of repentance, however, it still requires quite a leap to tie such repentance to the institution of *criminal punishment*. Should the very aim or purpose of punishment be to provoke repentance in the wrongdoer? Might this be, if not the primary aim, at least a permissible subordinate aim? If so, just how is punishment—the coercive infliction of *suffering*—supposed to accomplish this? (When people hurt me I tend to get angry and resentful, not remorseful.) And even if the purpose of punishment is not to provoke repentance, may such repentance—when it is found—legitimately affect such matters as sentencing, parole, clemency, and pardon? These are the questions to which I shall now turn.

Why do we punish? Most contemporary philosophical discussions of the justification of legal punishment see it as a practice driven mainly by two not totally consistent values: deterrence and retribution. Deterrence looks to the future and justifies the punishment of the criminal as an effective way of providing him with an incentive not to commit crime again (special deterrence) or of providing others who are aware of his punishment with an incentive not to commit crime at all (general deterrence).

Retribution, on the other hand, is not concerned with future consequences. Rather it looks to the past and seeks to impose on the criminal the level of suffering he *deserves*—that is, a level of suffering properly proportional to the wrongfulness of his criminal conduct.

Both of these justifications of punishment are problematic. Deterrence is open to the Kantian moral objection that it is willing to use people merely as means to produce social benefit and to the empirical objection that the law's capacity to deter may be more of a hope than a fact grounded in solid evidence.

Retribution is open to the conceptual objection that the concept of desert is difficult to analyze with any precision—indeed is perhaps little more than a metaphor left over from old theological notions of cosmic or divine justice—and that a just society will not impose suffering on people in pursuit of a mere metaphor. It also is not at all clear why the secular state—not in the business of playing God—should be concerned with punishing on the basis of moral desert anyway.

Problematic or not, the ideas of deterrence and retribution are likely to remain as the dominant contemporary justifications of punishment. Thus, for my present purposes, it will be useful to inquire into the degree to which, if at all, repentance fits comfortably within these justifications.

It might seem that, with respect to special deterrence, repentance has an important role to play; for it seems obvious that repentant people are less likely to commit crimes again than are those criminals who are unrepentant. Indeed, one might even suggest that controlling crime by provoking repentance is just another way of describing the idea of special deterrence.

This pattern of thought, though tempting, is hasty and superficial. Repentance surely means, not merely a resolution not to commit wrong again but a resolution that includes a desire to make amends and that is based on certain virtues of character—for example, *remorse* over the wrong that one has done. If one's concern in punishing is merely to deter future criminal conduct, however, then one may consistently (and perhaps would realistically) ask much less from punishment than this. Punishment as deterrence is essentially a system of *threats*, and threats appeal—not to the softer and more virtuous aspects of our character—but simply to our capacities for *fear* grounded in *self-interest*. The goal is social control, not moral and spiritual rebirth. Thus a deterrence justification of punishment might under certain circumstances welcome repentance as an extra incentive, but a rich concept of repentance—for example, one meaning more than merely being disinclined to commit crime again—will not be a central idea in such an outlook.

What about retribution? Do repentant people deserve less suffering that those who remain hard and unrepentant? Here we must distinguish two different versions of retributivism. According to what I will call *grievance retributivism*, punishment is deserved for responsible wrongful acts—acts that occasion legitimate grievances against the wrongdoer and that place the wrongdoer in a kind of debt to his victim and other fellow citizens.

According to what I will call *character retributivism*, one's deserts are a function not merely of one's wrongful acts but also of the ultimate state of one's character.

Repentance will have less obvious bearing on grievance retributivism than on character retributivism. In general, the wrongfulness of conduct at one time will not be affected by repentance at a later time. I typically do not cease to have a grievance against you simply because you are now sorry that you wronged me; nor do your debts to me disappear merely because you now lament those acts that put you into debt to me.

There are, however, some exceptions to this. Sometimes the wrongfulness of an act is a function of the harm that it brings to a victim, and sometimes this harm may be lessened through an act of repentance. This is because (as I have argued earlier) the harm experienced by the victim is sometimes (e.g., in some rapes) perceived in part as an insult or a degradation—the unwelcome message that the wrongdoer regards himself as superior to the victim and may use the victim, like a mere object, for his own purposes. Such an insulting message hurts; and this message may be withdrawn—and the hurt lessened—when the wrongdoer repents. This is why such repentance often opens the door to forgiveness; since, had forgiveness been granted earlier by the victim (prior to repentance by the wrongdoer), the victim might well fear that he was accepting—in a servile way—the insulting message contained in his victimization.

Often, of course, victims of wrongdoing will not see their hurt lessened by acts of repentance. Perhaps they will see the injury done (e.g., harms to their children, or harms that leave them with serious physical handicaps, or harms that leave them poor) as involving harms having little to do with insult or degradation, and thus will be unmoved by any change in "message" conveyed by the wrongdoer. Or perhaps they will see the injury and degradation they have suffered as being so grave as to be "unforgivable."

As Simon Wiesenthal asks in his book *The Sunflower*, how many Jews will be or should be moved by the difference between a repentant Nazi exterminator and an unrepentant Nazi exterminator? And if they are moved, in what direction will they be moved? Cynthia Ozick, in her essay in *The Sunflower*, suggests that the repentant Nazi reveals a moral nature that he must have repressed in order to engage in unspeakable practices. This, by her lights, makes him worse than someone who is simply a crude and unreflective thug and prompts Ozick to say of him: "Let him go to hell. Sooner the fly to God than he." Or consider Elie Wiesel's prayer at ceremonies marking the fiftieth anniversary in 1995 of the liberation of Auschwitz: "God of forgiveness, do not forgive those who created this place. God of mercy, have no mercy on those who killed here Jewish children."

In short: Although repentance may play some role around the edges, it will—at least initially—not seem central in those versions of retributivism that emphasize a concept of desert based mainly on wrongdoing, grievance, and debt.

What about those versions of retributivism that seek to target a concept of desert based not merely on wrongdoing but on ultimate character? Here repentance might well play a crucial role; for a repentant person seems to reveal a better character than an unrepentant person.

A concern with such nuances of character, however, is not likely to affect the basic design of the criminal code itself. Criminal punishment is, after all, an exercise of political or state power. It is easy to see why such power will be mainly concerned with wrongdoing (either to prevent it or to give it what it deserves, in the sense of removing a debt or righting a wrong) but hard to see why the state—particularly the liberal secular state—should be concerned with ultimate character independent of wrongdoing. It would seem that it could at most address this concern as a subordinate goal—perhaps as a way of constraining, through fine-tuned individuation, a system mainly concerned with other matters. Thus it is not surprising that, in a legal world dominated by the values of deterrence and politically relevant retribution (i.e., grievance retribution), a concern with issues of deep character will more likely be regarded as relevant, if at all, at the level of sentencing or pardon or restoration of rights for parolees (issues to be discussed later in the chapter) than at the level of the basic design and purpose of the criminal code itself.

It was not always this way, of course. Plato, although he made some place for general deterrence and incapacitation in his account of punishment in his great dialogue *Laws*, rejected retribution (which he could not distinguish from mindless vengeance) as utterly barbaric. He offered instead, as the dominant value that should govern criminal punishment, the value of *moral improvement*—punishment as a means of transforming the character of the criminal from a state of vice to a state of virtue. The goal of punishment is future oriented, but not mainly as a device for securing future compliance to law. Compliance is not the primary aim of punishment but will rather be secured as a by-product of the value that is the primary aim: instilling in the criminal not just a fear based in self-interest but rather a true sense of justice—a desire to do the right thing for the right reason. The goal is to confer on the criminal a good (the greatest good: a good character), and this is why the theory is sometimes referred to as a "paternalistic" theory of punishment.

This Platonic theory, until recently rejected by legal philosophers as quite implausible, has now been powerfully resurrected—particularly in the recent writings of R. A. Duff, Herbert Morris, and Jean Hampton. Since repentance has a central role to play in such a theory—particularly in Duff's version—it will be useful to consider it in this discussion.

First of all, it is worth considering why—for a long time—the theory that punishment may function to generate repentance was understandably rejected as implausible. There are several reasons. The most obvious is that our primary methods of punishment are so brutal as to make repentance either impossible or unlikely. (In spite of Dr. Johnson's quip that the prospect of being hanged tends to focus the mind, the death penalty and incarceration in the pesthole that is the modern jail and prison seem primarily to brutalize all those who come in contact with the system.) In addition, contemporary criminal law (at least in America) tends toward radical overcriminalization—punishing many offenses with absurd excess and regarding some actions as crimes that, since their moral wrongness is doubtful, are also doubtful objects of repentance. The Georgia penal code, for example, provides that consensual homosexual sodomy may be punished by up to twenty years in prison, but it is by no means obvious that the homosexual has done evil of a kind for which repentance may legitimately be demanded by a secular community. In addition, the criminal process will sometimes result in the conviction of persons who are actually innocent. To demand repentance of such persons is simply to add insult to the injury that they suffer from being unjustly punished. Consider finally the crimes (for example, criminal trespass, unlawful assembly) that may be committed by persons whose motives are those of nonviolent civil disobedience. Do we really want to seek repentance from the Martin Luther King Jr.s and Gandhis of the world?

The answer to these worries is, I think, to insist that the paternalistic theory of punishment is an *ideal* theory—not a description of the world in which we live but rather the portrait of a world to which we might aspire. A state or community properly using the criminal law to provoke repentance would have only just laws (laws organized around a respect for fundamental human rights) and would use only methods of punishment that would assist genuine moral rebirth and not simply reflex conformity or terrified submission. Thus the fact that most of our present penal practices are not of this nature will be seen—by someone committed to the paternalistic theory—as a condemnation of those practices and not as a refutation of the paternalistic theory itself. The Chinese demand for criminal repentance under the regime of Mao was morally disgusting not because it sought repentance for a violation of community norms but because the norms themselves were often very evil and the means used to secure repentance were degrading.

Even as an ideal theory, however, the paternalistic theory is open to serious challenge. Punishments that are not brutal and inhumane must still, if they are truly to be called punishments, inflict some serious deprivation—some hard treatment—on offenders. (Otherwise how would punishment be distinguished from reward or from psychiatric therapy as a means of reform?) How is this hard treatment to be justified as a step toward repentance and reform?

There is, of course, an obvious connection between repentance and suffering. Repentant people feel *guilty*, and a part of feeling guilty is a sense that one ought to suffer punishment. Thus guilty and repentant people may well seek out, or at least accept willingly, the punishment that is appropriate for their wrongdoing.

This connection, by itself, will not yield the paternalistic theory, however. For the connection thus far establishes only that repentance will naturally lead to an accepting of punishment (or other penance). The paternalistic theory, however, requires that the connection go in the other direction—that is, that punishment itself will produce repentance. How could this be so?

There is a traditional answer here, but it is not one that is likely to appeal to the contemporary mind. A certain kind of Platonist, committed to soul/body dualism, might argue that tendencies to wrongdoing arise from the desires of the body when those desires are not under the proper control of the rational soul.

St. Paul was no doubt under the influence of this kind of Platonism when, in Romans 8:23, he described his own moral failings by saying "I see another law in my members, warring against the law of my mind, and bringing me into captivity to the law of sin which is in my members." Given such a view, it is not difficult to imagine that the infliction of suffering that mortifies the body might well cause one to grow to hate the body and focus more on the soul and the life of virtue that the soul makes possible.

Such an account is, of course, highly problematic. It is hard for the contemporary mind to embrace a sharp soul/body dualism and even harder to accept the claim that wrongdoing typically arises from desires of the body. (This may work for rape, but it seems highly implausible for treason.) Some vice is highly intellectual in nature and results far more from a corrupt mind or will than from slavery to the body. Thus, if one wants a theory that follows in Plato's spirit without embracing the metaphysics of his letter, one might see punishment as reforming—not merely by subjecting the body—but by curtailing the power of whatever aspect of the personality is responsible for vice. As Herbert Fingarette has argued, the wrongdoer has assumed a power greater than is his right to assume, and thus it is important that he have his will humbled. Punishment makes him suffer (in the sense of *endure*), and such suffering gives him not only what he deserves but also provides him with an important lesson in the legitimate scope of his power.

But how does punishment itself make the lesson *take*? Unless we can imagine a plausible mechanism to explain how the infliction of suffering itself generates repentance and reform, it looks as though we will at most be able to claim that punishment provides us with an *opportunity* to do *something else* to a person (provide therapy, education, religious instruction, etc.) that might be reformative. But then we would be justifying punishment not in terms of its own reformative potential but simply in terms of the opportunities that it provides—hardly the challenging promise originally held out by the paternalistic theory.

R. A. Duff is sensitive to this problem and makes a very promising start toward salvaging the paternalistic theory from the many objections that have been raised against it. He makes no pretense that punishment can guarantee repentance and reform. (Neither, of course, can other interventions—for example, psychotherapy—that also aim at reform.) In this sense he would agree that punishment can do no more than offer criminals an opportunity for moral rebirth. In his view, however, the opportunity is presented by the punishment itself and not by some other devices that might be employed while punishment is being endured.

How could this be? It is, claims Duff, because punishment must be understood in *communitarian* terms—as an *act of communication* between the community and a person who has flouted one of that community's shared norms. The suffering endured is that of separation from a valued community—a community that the criminal values (perhaps without realizing it until he experiences its loss) and to which he would like to return—and communicates to the wrongdoer the judgment that his actions have made him, at least temporarily, unworthy of full participation in the life of the community. It requires that he experience the pain of separation so that he can come to see, in his heart, the appropriateness of that separation and thus seek, with the appropriate humility, reconciliation with the community that he has wronged. In other words, the hope is that a kind of compulsory penance will be replaced by a voluntary penance. Voluntary penance is a sincere act of reattachment or allegiance to community values—an act that will allow the wrongdoer to be welcomed again and reintegrated into community life. And what makes this paternalistic? Simply this: Punishment on such terms will benefit the wrongdoer because severance from a community—if it is a *just* and *decent* community—is a genuine harm to the individual who is isolated, and reintegration is a genuine good for him.

According to Duff, the *right sort* of prison may help the wrongdoer to achieve the good of reintegration because it removes the criminal from his corrupting peers, and provides the opportunity for and the stimulus to a reflective self-examination which will ideally induce repentance and self-reform. Also worth considering are such alternatives to prison as community service and restitution.

Duff's theory is rich and in many ways compelling. It cannot be the whole story on the justification of punishment, but it is—in my judgment—an important and largely neglected part of the story. It may, of course, be highly unrealistic to attempt an application of the theory to the crime problem in a society such as that found in contemporary America. It is not at all clear to what degree there is a genuine community of values in our society; and even where there may be a community of values, it is sometimes the case that those who flout those values feel so alienated (perhaps because of poverty or racial injustice or cultural exclusion) that they could not reasonably see reintegration into the community as a good to be secured by their punishment, because they never felt truly integrated into the community in the first place. However, if the paternalistic theory really is a compelling ideal theory, then even a serious gap between theory and practice will not be a legitimate ground for rejecting the theory. Rather it will be an occasion for mourning the community that we have lost and for seeking to regain it—or for seeking to create it if we have never had it. Those committed to the paternalistic view will argue that we should work to create a community of mutual concern and respect wherein punishment, if needed at all, could—without self-deception or hypocrisy—be defended on paternalistic grounds.

But suppose that we are sufficiently charmed by the paternalistic theory that we want to get started now and not wait for the ideal world. How might we proceed? Perhaps the best arena in which initially to attempt to apply the theory is to be found, not in the adult criminal law but in the law dealing with juvenile offenders. Juvenile offenders are probably more open to radical character transformations than are adults. In addition, the more informal and discretionary proceedings might allow—in encounters between offender (and family) and victim (and family)—the use of empathy to build a sense of community that more abstract and formal proceedings might mask.

It is also possible that one might be able to draw on subcommunities in ways that would ultimately benefit the larger community by developing in juvenile offenders a sense of self-worth through "belonging." For example, in 1994 a state court in Washington placed the punishment of two Tlingit teenagers guilty of robbery and assault in the hands of a tribal court—a court that banished the teenagers for eighteen months to separate uninhabited Alaskan islands in the hope that the necessity of surviving on their own, with only traditional tools and folkways to guide them, would build their characters and allow them reintegration into the community. Ideally, of course, one would want all citizens to feel a sense of belonging in the larger national community. One has to start somewhere, however, and—since self-esteem cannot grow in an asocial vacuum—why not (before gangs come in and assume the role) take advantage of the opportunities offered by particular cultural sub-groups? Such experiments are surely worth a try—even though the Tlingit experiment failed, alas, when friends and family intervened in unhelpful ways.

In this world, of course, we will no doubt continue to employ a system of criminal punishment that is driven by a variety of different values. Even if we seek to introduce paternalistic concerns as one of our justifications, concerns with crime control (deterrence and incapacitation) and retribution will also loom large. In a system driven by these nonpaternalistic values, even full repentance on the part of the criminal will frequently be viewed as not sufficient to remove the need for punishment. Punishing even the fully repentant might well serve general deterrence values, and it almost certainly will be demanded by crime victims who believe, on grievance retributive grounds, that the injuries that they have suffered require a response that is proportional to the wrongs that have produced those injuries.

If repentance is to play any role at all in our present system of criminal punishment, then, it will probably be as one reason bearing on whatever *discretion* officials are allowed within a punitive range that satisfies the legitimate demands of crime control and grievance retribution. If, for example, we have grounds for believing that society's legitimate general deterrence and retributive objectives with respect to a specific offense could be satisfied by any punishment within a particular range (e.g., three to eight years), then sincere repentance could provide an authority with discretion (normally a sentencing judge or an executive with the power of pardon) with a good reason for choosing a punishment at the lower rather than the higher end of the range. I shall refer to decisions to impose a reduced sentence as acts of mercy when they are based on some relevant aspect of the offender rather than on factors of a purely external nature, such as jail overcrowding.

But in what sense is repentance a relevant aspect? The obvious answer is to be found within the context of what I earlier called character retributivism. The repentant person has a better character than the un-repentant person, and thus the repentant person—on this theory—simply deserves less punishment than the unrepentant person. This basis for mercy—meaning here simply a reduction of sentence—is easy to understand, and may even be conceptualized as an aspect of justice.

Less immediately apparent, however, is a way that repentance can be a basis for mercy (again as sentence reduction) even within the context of what I earlier called grievance retributivism. Victims of wrongdoing are often vindictive and want the person who wronged them to suffer. If these victims are moral and rational, however, they will not desire that the wrongdoer suffer to any degree greater than he deserves.

But what is deserved suffering? I have neither the space nor the talent to present a complete theory of this matter here, but one thing should be obvious: If the concept of deserved suffering makes any sense at all, then the concept of deserved suffering will to a considerable degree be a function of the overall *amount* of suffering that the wrongdoer experiences.

We normally expect the proper amount of suffering to be administered by the state through legal punishment. However, if there is reason to believe that the individual has already experienced a significant amount of relevant suffering through nonlegal channels, it is not unreasonable to suggest that the suffering he experience at the hands of the state be reduced to that degree—perhaps eliminated entirely in those cases where we are inclined to say "he has suffered enough." If mercy—in the sense of reduction of legal punishment—is extended on these grounds, this will not compromise the legitimate claims of grievance retributivism but will instead be required by them.

Of course, not all suffering is relevant—for example, not the suffering (e.g., loss of professional reputation) that a wrongdoer might experience from losing a position that his criminal conduct showed that he had no right to enjoy in the first place.

I am inclined to think that the suffering that one imposes on oneself through repentance is very different from this, however. The sincerely repentant person tortures himself—hates at least that aspect of himself that allowed him to engage in the wrong he now laments—and the pain that this produces is arguably relevant in a way that a painful loss of an undeserved honorific status is not. Unless the victim's injury is one that is regarded as simply unforgivable, then the self-generated suffering experienced by the repentant wrongdoer might well be accepted by an aggrieved victim as a part of what he is owed in the way of suffering from the person who wronged him. If he does not accept this, then it would seem that the burden of argument now shifts to him to explain why, if the amount of relevant suffering is proper, it matters in any deep moral sense what percentage of it comes from the state.

We can now see how repentance could be a basis for sentence reduction even on grievance retributive grounds. The actual use of this basis, however, is tricky. We normally consider granting mercy or pardon when someone begs or petitions for it. A truly repentant person, however, would normally see his suffering punishment as *proper* and might, as noted earlier, even seek it out. Why then is he begging for mercy and trying to avoid more punishment? Is the fact that he wants us to reduce his punishment perhaps evidence that he is not repentant; and are we then faced with the problem that the only persons who are truly eligible for mercy on grounds of repentance will almost never get it because their repentance will cause them not to ask for it?

There are reasons for being cautious here, and many practical problems of distinguishing real from counterfeit repentance exist. In my judgment, however, there are no insoluble problems of principle. And this is for two reasons. First, we might have sufficient grounds to grant mercy in cases where the person (perhaps because of neurotic desires for too much self-punishment) refuses to ask for it. Second, if we take the trouble to inquire, we might find that some repentant persons ask for mercy, not so that they can avoid some deserved suffering but in order that they can leave prison and do something useful and good with what remains of their lives. We should not simply assume that all such expressions are disguises for self-interest, although some of them certainly are.

In summary: A truly repentant wrongdoer is recommitted to community values, requires no additional special deterrence, and clearly—on the theory of character retributivism—deserves less punishment than a wrongdoer who is unrepentant. When one could promote the goods represented by these considerations without compromising the law's legitimate interest in crime control and grievance retribution (to which repentance, I have argued, may also be relevant), it would seem irrational—even cruel—not to do so and bestow mercy.

There are, of course, degrees of mercy; and the grounds that justify letting a person out of prison may not require that the community treat the freed individual exactly as he would have been treated prior to any criminal conduct. The heavyweight champion Mike Tyson served his sentence for rape and was properly released from prison. The football and movie star O. J. Simpson, charged with murdering his wife and her friend, was acquitted at trial and was properly released from prison. Substantial segments of the American public refuse to welcome these two men back into American society, however, because they are viewed as wrongdoers who refuse to acknowledge and repent of their wrongdoing. Although both men maintain their innocence, many people simply do not believe them and thus, while agreeing that they must be freed from jail, still refuse to accord them their previous levels of respect—for example, by no longer employing them for commercial endorsements.

And consider the case of Tonya Harding. She did express remorse for what she claimed to be her limited role in the criminal assault on fellow Olympic skater Nancy Kerrigan, but the American public—while no doubt generally content with the plea bargain that allowed her to avoid jail time—still continues to treat her with contempt. Is this because of a belief that she minimized her actual role in the crime, or a belief that she is not truly repentant, or an unwillingness to forgive her even if she is truly repentant? There is no way of knowing for sure; and I mention this and the previous cases simply to make the point that "We will let you out of jail" often does not lead to "We will fully welcome you back into the community." No doubt the former generally should lead to the latter; but sometimes there are perhaps understandable reasons why it does not.

The reentry problems faced by Tyson, Simpson, and Harding are, of course, mainly concerned with the private responses that other citizens choose to make to them—responses (e.g., refusals to offer opportunities for commercial endorsements) that are clearly within the rights of those citizens.

But what if it is the *state* that refuses to allow—even for the repentant and freed criminal—full reentry into the rights and privileges of society? Even this, I think, is a matter of considerable complexity.

Consider the issue of the restoration of certain rights to paroled felons—a matter that, in the absence of specific legislative enactments, is often left in the hands of officials of state agencies that are neither judicial nor executive.

For example: A few years ago, the admissions committee of the College of Law at my university admitted a paroled murderer into the first-year class. The outcry from alumni and legislators was enormous—including a realistic threat to withdraw funding from the college and shut it down. Both the parole board and the admissions committee believed that the individual, who had served a very long prison term, was sincerely repentant, fully rehabilitated, and desired to make the rest of his life of some use to society. Critics regarded this argument as irrelevant either because they doubted the sincerity of the repentance or, more commonly, because they believed that even fully repentant murderers owed a lifetime debt to their victims and to the community that could not be overcome by any change of character.

Who is right here? It is, I think, very hard to say. Although I supported and continue to support the admission of this person to the College of Law, the decision was a close call for me because I think that reasonable people can be on either side of an issue of this nature. Even those who advocate reintegration of repentant criminals into the community might have reasonable grounds for limiting this reintegration. Although it would surely be unconscionable to deny such individuals access to state medical care or even general state programs of university education, it does not strike me as comparably unconscionable to adopt, if not an absolute rule, at least a strong presumption against allowing such individuals access to such a scarce and costly community resource as a tax-funded legal education.

What this discussion shows, I think, is that much more thinking needs to be done on the relationship between mercy and repentance. Repentance may earn a reduction in sentence—perhaps even a full release from prison—but may understandably be viewed as not sufficient to earn complete reintegration into the community. It may get you out of the fire and into the frying pan, but—as I think J. L. Austin remarked somewhere—it may be a frying pan that is still in a fire.

I close this chapter by returning to the issue of collective repentance. When one thinks of repentance in connection with criminal punishment, one tends to think that all demands for repentance must be addressed to the criminal. But surely the community, through its patterns of abuse, neglect and discrimination, sometimes creates a social environment that undermines the development of virtuous character and makes the temptations to crime very great—greater than many of us might have been able to resist if similarly situated.

The important idea here is not that criminals, if they are from social groups that are poor or despised or abused or discriminated against, are not to any degree responsible for their criminality. They are. As a part of their dignity as human beings, they must be seen as responsible agents and not merely as helpless victims. But their responsibility is, in my view, sometimes *shared* with those of us in the larger community. In these cases, we too may be legitimately called on for repentance and atonement—attitudes of mind that should prevent us from thinking of criminals as monsters—as beings totally different from us—and should thus moderate our tendencies to respond to them with nothing but malice.

At present, however, unrepentant viciousness toward criminals has become an increasingly pervasive feature of American society. So out of control is this passion that Judge Richard A. Posner, hardly a bleeding-heart sentimentalist, powerfully condemned it one of his judicial opinions:

There are different ways to look on the inmates of prisons and jails in the United States in 1995. One way is to look on them as members of a different species, indeed as a type of vermin, devoid of human dignity and entitled to no respect. . . .

I do not myself consider the 1.5 million inmates of American prisons and jails in that light. This is a non-negligible fraction of the American population. And it is only the current inmate population. The fraction of the total population that has spent time in a prison or jail is larger. . . . A substantial number of these prison and jail inmates . . . have not been convicted of a crime. They are merely charged with crime, and awaiting trial. Some of them may actually be innocent. Of the guilty, many are guilty of sumptuary offenses, or of other victimless crimes uncannily similar to lawful activity (gambling offenses are an example), or of esoteric financial and regulatory offenses (such as violation of the migratory game laws) some of which do not even require a guilty intent. It is wrong to break even foolish laws, or wise laws that should carry only civil penalties. It is wrongful to break the law when the lawbreaker is flawed, weak, retarded, unstable, ignorant, brutalized, or profoundly disadvantaged, rather than violent, vicious, or evil to the core. But we should have a realistic conception of the composition of the prison and jail population before deciding that they are scum entitled to nothing better than what a vengeful populace and a resource-starved penal system choose to give them. We must not exaggerate the distance between "us," the lawful ones, the respectable ones, and the prison and jail population; for such exaggeration will make it too easy for us to deny that population the rudiments of humane consideration. (*Johnson v. Phelan*, 7th Circuit U.S. Court of Appeals, 1995)

Although I have argued that mercy and forgiveness are in some important ways different virtues, they are both related in at least this way: they are both more likely to emerge in a person who has *compassion*. When compassion is lacking, however, neither will receive much of a hearing.

Even though there are good reasons why we cannot always grant mercy—just as there are good reasons why we cannot always forgive—I think we should always at least be open to it, even disposed toward it, because, at some level, we all require it and should hope that our repentance might be seen as a ground for it.

Annie, in the novel *Mr. Ives' Christmas* by Oscar Hijuelos, maintained that "in her opinion the troubles in life were started by people who never looked into their own souls." All of us would be well advised to take her advice to heart and, as we demand repentance of the criminal, demand it also of ourselves. If we find that we are unwilling or unable to demand it of ourselves, perhaps we should conclude that we have forfeited our right to demand it from the criminal.

SIX

SELF-FORGIVENESS

I first began to think about self-forgiveness in conversations with the late Jean Hampton when we were writing *Forgiveness and Mercy*.

My relations with Jean were generally that of friendly adversary. We disagreed on a great deal—her Christianity against my then (but not now) militantly secular worldview, her assumptions of trust and love against my more cautious and even cynical assumptions, her refusal to endorse the vindictive feelings that seemed (at least in some circumstances) so very right to me. And yet we agreed on a great deal as well—for example, our shared belief that some form of retribution has an important role to play in the practice of criminal punishment, although Jean wanted to distinguish retribution from vengeance more sharply than I did.

Self-forgiveness is an "in" topic these days—much discussed in both academic and popular psychology, filling the shelves of the self-help and recovery sections of chain bookstores, and playing a prominent role in various twelve-step programs. It might be useful to see what, if anything, philosophy can contribute to its understanding. I should make it clear at the outset, however, that I have no final and original account of my own to offer of self-forgiveness. I hope, however, that I will at least be able to point out some false starts and suggest what will *not* work.

What are the reasons that might legitimately prompt one to forgive a person by whom one has been deeply wronged? In the book I wrote with Jean, I stressed (as I have here) mainly reasons of a self-regarding nature—particularly the fact that forgiveness can legitimately allow one to get on with one's life *if* one can find a way to bestow it consistent with one's self-respect, as one frequently can if the wrongdoer manifests sincere repentance. I gave short shrift—one brief paragraph—to the possible effects of forgiveness on the wrongdoer himself. I considered the possibility that forgiveness might be justified as part of an attempt to reform the wrongdoer, but then rejected this as arrogant and patronizing. I wrote:

> Suppose you had wronged someone. How would you like it if that person assumed that you could not come to repentance on your own but required the aid of his ministry of forgiveness? Might you not feel patronized—condescended to? Forgiveness can be an act of weakness, but it can also be an act of arrogance. Seeing it in this way, the wrongdoer might well resent the forgiveness. "Who do you think you are to forgive me?" he might respond to such well-meaning meddling. (Murphy and Hampton, 1988, p. 31)

Jean sharply disagreed with me on this point. Indeed, she closed her chapter on forgiveness by suggesting that the good that forgiveness can bring to the wrongdoer constitutes one of the *best* reasons justifying forgiveness. She wrote:

> [P]erhaps the greatest good forgiveness can bring is the liberation of the wrongdoer from the effects of the victim's moral hatred. . . . [Such forgiveness] may enable wrongdoers to forgive themselves by showing them that there is still enough decency in them to warrant renewed association with them. It may save them from the hell of self-loathing. (Murphy and Hampton, 1988, pp. 86–87)

I did not explore this disagreement in the book—she had already given me too much else to think about—and so I welcome the opportunity to explore it here. I will in particular be concerned with three questions: What is self-forgiveness? Under what circumstances is self-forgiveness a good? How might forgiveness from another (one's victim of earlier wrongdoing) bring about self-forgiveness?

If one literally follows Bishop Butler's famous analysis of forgiveness, then the idea of self-forgiveness might seem incoherent. It will be recalled that, according to Butler, forgiveness essentially involves the overcoming of *resentment*, and it seems bizarre to speak of resenting oneself.

I have now been persuaded by Norvin Richards and others, however, that it is a mistake to define forgiveness so narrowly. It is more illuminating—more loyal to the actual texture of our moral lives—to think of forgiveness as overcoming a variety of negative feelings that one might have toward a wrongdoer—resentment, yes, but also such feelings as anger, hatred, loathing, contempt, indifference, disappointment, or even sadness. There is no reason to think that even this list is complete.

Some of these feelings, of course, make perfectly good sense to ascribe to oneself. The concepts of self-hatred or self-loathing, for example, are perfectly coherent in a way that self-resentment perhaps is not. And thus it is a step in the right direction that Hampton organizes her thinking about self-forgiveness around these concepts. She wrote:

> If the wrongdoer [sees himself as] cloaked in evil, or as infected with moral rot, [this] can engender moral hatred of himself. Such self-loathing is the feeling that he is, entirely or in part, morally hideous, unclean, infected. It can be directed at his character or dispositions or, more dangerously, towards everything that he is, so that he comes to believe that there is nothing good or decent in him. . . . [This] can lead to self-destruction. (Murphy and Hampton, 1988, p. 86)

The particular kind of self-hatred that interests Hampton here is most forcefully expressed by the other phrase that she uses in this passage: *moral hatred* of oneself. One can, of course, hate oneself for reasons having little or nothing to do with morality—for exmple, Nancy Snow's example of the football player who is overcome with self-loathing over dropping a pass that would have, if completed, won the game for his team. This player may need to attain self-forgiveness if he is ever to get on with his life, but nonmoral cases such as this are not the ones of central interest here. The self-hatred felt by the player is not moral hatred; and it is moral hatred that is the object of present concern.

But what exactly does this phrase "moral hatred" mean? Earlier in the book, Hampton defined moral hatred—in contrast to simple hatred—in this way:

> An aversion to someone who has identified himself with an immoral cause or practice, prompted by moral indignation and accompanied by the wish to triumph over him and his cause or practice in the name of some fundamental moral principle or objective, most notably justice. (Murphy and Hampton, 1988, p. 61)

This definition will not quite do, of course, with respect to moral hatred of self; for once again—as noted earlier with respect to resentment—one often finds oneself in confusion when one attempts to transfer language from interpersonal relations to relations to oneself. Can one, for example, really feel *indignation* toward oneself?

I think that perhaps the best way to understand moral hatred of self is as a kind of *shame* placed on top of guilt: guilt over what one has done but, in cases where being a moral person is a part of what Freud would call one's ego ideal, shame that one has fallen so far below one's ideal of selfhood that life—at least life with full self-consciousness—is now less bearable. This kind of shame, so visual in its imagery, is well captured in the idea that one needs, at the end of the day, to be able to look at oneself in the mirror and that, after certain moral failings, one simply would find it difficult to do so. Oedipus's blinding of himself is, of course, the most famous literary example of this kind of self-loathing.

But what is it about *moral* failures that could generate such shameful hatred or self-loathing? How do we understand moral failures in such a way that one could plausibly loathe or hate oneself for them? We do not typically feel this way about our aesthetic failures (my inability to write fiction of literary value, for example), nor would self-loathing be a feeling that one would expect to find in persons whose moral outlook was totally utilitarian in nature. Self-loathing seems to require a rich (almost Dostoevskian) account of morality that regards the *past* with deadly seriousness and makes *character* (in some rich sense) a central element. What might such an account look like?

Jean did not attempt to develop a full account of immorality in our book—although she did give some hints—but she did so at some length in her later writings. I now want to examine this account in order to determine if it will provide an adequate foundation for a concept of moral self-hatred or self-loathing that will illuminate self-forgiveness.

Drawing on relevant theological and philosophical traditions, Hampton claims that the essential feature of the concept of immorality is *defiance*, defiance of the rules of morality. She speaks in a similar way in the book where she refers to the immoral person as in *rebellion* against morality and speaks of the object of moral hatred as aversion to one who has *identified himself* with an unjust cause. In later essays, however, the view is spelled out in much more detail in passages such as the following:

> The explanation [of immorality] I will develop is naturally linked with the idea that the authority of moral imperatives comes from the idea that they are categorical. I call it the *defiance*

explanation, it is very old, deeply entrenched in the Judeo-Christian tradition, and implicit in the tale of Adam and Eve, which is supposed to be an explanation of the origin of human evil. (Hampton, 1989, p. 34)

The point of the tale [is that] human immorality is a function of human disobedience of an authoritative command. . . . In a nutshell, the view is that a culpable agent is one who chooses to defy what she knows to be an authoritative moral command in the name of the satisfaction of one or more of her wishes, whose satisfaction the command forbids. (Hampton, 1990, pp. 14–15)

Hampton claims that her defiance account of immorality is inspired by Milton's idea in *Paradise Lost* of "foul revolt" and by Kant's account of evil in *Religion Within the Limits of Reason Alone*—where (according to Hampton's controversial interpretation) Kant sees immorality as arising from insubordination by one who defies the Moral Law and puts the satisfaction of his own desires ahead of doing his duty. One of the great virtues of this defiance account, she claims, is that

[it explicates] the notion [of immorality] as it functions in our everyday judgments and practices . . . [and] explains the kinds of reactive attitudes we have towards wrongdoers. Insofar as it presents immoral actions as chosen by a person . . . it makes sense to respond negatively to the person who made the choices. . . . We who are (supposedly) on the side of morality find the wrongdoer's rebellious choices offensive. She is not someone to be pitied, but someone to be resented, resisted, fought against, or even despised because of her allegiance. . . . [The wrongdoer herself might come to feel] shame, a kind of misery over what one is (a traitor to the right cause). (Hampton, 1989, pp. 41–42)

Is Hampton right about all of this? I do not think so.

But how does one argue against a theory of this nature? I think that all one can do is test the theory introspectively—against one's own moral psychology—and, if the two do not match, share such exercises in psychological autobiography with others to see if they too find that the theory produces tension rather than coherence. Hampton herself invites such an approach when she says that her theory captures "our" reactive attitudes, how "we" tend to feel. How can one, as a critic, respond to such a claim except by confessing "not me; this is not how *I* feel." One puts such a confession forward as a wager that others will share one's dissent from the offered analysis. The wager is dangerous, of course, because if others do not share one's dissent one discovers that one's own moral psychology is idiosyncratic or even pathological. With this caution in mind, I will now place my bet.

I suppose that my primary quarrel with Hampton's account is its high level of formality and generality—a product, I suspect, of its Kantian origins. (Kant believed that the essence of immorality is to be found in the willful violation of moral rules.) I can understand regarding some immorality as explained by the abstract concepts of "authoritative commands" and "the Moral Law," but I cannot for a moment imagine *hating* or *loathing* myself for sins of such an abstract nature. The immoralities for which I (and I suspect most of us) have felt and still feel some self-loathing are those that come with specific names and specific faces attached to them—the faces of those who were victims of one's hurtful conduct. Defiance of rules alone, I suspect, simply will not—for most normal people—yield this result.

Consider again the story of Adam and Eve—a story to which Hampton devotes several pages of close discussion in developing her defiance theory. In my view, one misses a great deal that is important in the story if one sees it—as Hampton does—as essentially a story about the defiance of categorical moral authority. After all, the discussion between Eve and the serpent focuses not on issues that Kant would recognize as issues of moral principle but rather on competing prudential hypotheses—on what Kant would call competing hypothetical imperatives. Eve seems concerned not with God's abstract moral authority but rather with the question of the reliability of God's promise to sustain her being and promote her interests. She fears to eat from the tree not because she has some primitive grasp that "Do not eat from the tree" is a categorical imperative but because God has said that anyone who does eat from the tree will die. She is not sure, however, that her fear is justified; and thus the serpent is able to seduce her into disobedience, not by inviting her to replace God's moral authority with her own but rather by reassuring her about the promised sanction. He says simply "Of course you will not die," and Eve, alas, believes him. In my view, what the serpent blinds Eve from seeing is not the majesty of God's categorical moral authority but rather the fact that God knows what is in the best interest of his creatures—a point missed by an overly Kantian reading of the story. The God of the story is to be obeyed for the very practical and prudential reason that he created human beings and therefore knows what is required in order for them to flourish.

I think that an overly Kantian reading also makes us miss an aspect of the story that is even more important for my present purposes—the nature of any shame and guilt that Adam and Eve feel after their disobedience. Their dominant feelings following the disobedience are, of course, not moral at all. Their feelings are rather the feelings of pain and insecurity that come with the realization that they are now irrevocably worse off than they were before; life is going to be hard. They do also, however, experience the moral feelings of shame and perhaps guilt. And what is the basis for these feelings? At least with respect to their shame, this seems to have as its object not defiance but rather some *knowledge* that they have acquired as a result of their defiance: the knowledge that they are naked. If they also experience guilt (and the story does not tell us that they do) is this because they have defied an authoritative rule or rather because they have deeply and obviously betrayed and disappointed—and thus *hurt*—the Heavenly Father who loves them? I suspect it is in large part the latter. God's response to them strikes me as personal as well; it is largely that of an injured but still loving father whose loving care has been unappreciated, not simply the response of a cosmic policeman or judge who—like Oliver Wendell Holmes, Jr.— holds the abstract belief that the law must keep its promises. The story of the garden is a powerful *personal* drama and a powerful *family* drama, and the replacement of God the Father by the impersonal categorical imperative would, I think, be a nontrivial modification in the story.

I am supported in this hunch by, if I understand him correctly, Bernard Williams. He has argued—in his book *Shame and Necessity*— that Western guilt morality (in contrast to shame morality) had, at the time of its origins, one great strength: attention to the hurts and claims of victims. He claims that the strength was lost, however, when guilt morality became overly Kantian—that is, highly abstract and formal. The worry that Williams raises about guilt morality in general applies, I think, to the Kantianism of Hampton's particular analysis of immorality. The powerful claims of victims—their hurts, their outrages, even their hatreds—drop out in favor of an abstract concept of defiance to law. What drops out as well (I suspect) are the powerful reactive attitudes that seem so naturally a part of either being a victim or reacting to victims but so artificially grafted on to abstract notions of law. If, as Hampton claims, her goal is in part to explain our ordinary reactive attitudes to wrongdoers, then the defiance theory—in my judgment—fails to provide such an explanation.

If the essence of immorality is defiance of the rules, of the moral law, then we should feel the same amount of shame and guilt in all cases of wrongful defiance—regardless of whether anyone is hurt by that defiance. But we do not; this is simply not the way we are wired.

Let me return to the issue of self-hatred and the need for self-forgiveness and pursue in that context the issue of "moral luck"—an issue discussed earlier in the context of Supreme Court opinions on victim impact statements. A normal person who drives while intoxicated and kills a child in a crosswalk will, I suspect, feel self-hatred for a long time—perhaps unto death. But the same person probably will not feel self-hatred if, through good luck, there is no child in the crosswalk when he speeds through it. In the first scenario, the person may spend a lifetime searching in vain for self-forgiveness, whereas in the second scenario the person would hardly see the point of even raising the issue. The difference here can only be explained by the presence of harm in the one case and the absence of harm in the other; the element of defiance—if it is present at all—is the same in both.

Our reactive attitudes simply are what they are, and any theory that purports—as Hampton's does—to "explain the kinds of reactive attitudes we have towards wrongdoers as [these attitudes] function in our everyday judgments and practices" must explain them as they are—not as they would be if we were programmed in a more Protestant-Kantian way.

Let me sum up my critique of Hampton to this point: I think that the kind of self-hatred that Hampton calls moral hatred (a kind of hatred in need of self-forgiveness) cannot be explained by her defiance view of immorality. We typically hate ourselves not because of such abstract and formal violations of moral rules but because we see vividly the harm that we have inflicted on others by such violations. Indeed, although some Kantians hate to admit it, the nature of the harm often enters into the explanation of the severity of the violation. Robust defiance of major rules will often, in the absence of injury, leave us free—if not of all negative emotions of self-assessment—at least of such heavy ones as self-loathing and self-hatred. Knowing or even merely thoughtless neglect of lesser rules, however, will often generate self-hatred if we see that such neglect inflicts injury—particularly injury on those with whom we are intimately involved and about whom we care deeply. The writer A. N. Wilson captures this point nicely in the following passage from his novel *Incline Our Hearts*.

It is only on those whom I have loved that I have ever knowingly inflicted pain. The guilt of it remains for ever, my words selected with such malice and the startled expression on the victim's face as the effect went home. These are the faces which return during nights of insomnia, forever hurt in my memories, and inconsolably so. It is said that time is a healer, but it is not necessarily so. Memory has the power to encapsulate moments of pain, to freeze them, so that though the person who suffered has drifted on into other worlds and other states of feeling or non-feeling, the remembered moments of pain can stay. Sometimes in spells of profound depression, it is these moments alone which surface in the memory. Everything else is a bland, misty background against which these figures stand out sharp and clear—women in tears, or my uncle, drawing back the corner of his lips and sticking a pipe in his mouth, trying to conceal the extent to which I was hurting him. (Wilson, 1990, pp. 143–144)

Wilson here captures perfectly at least my sense of the paradigm cases where self-hatred is likely to arise and thus where self-forgiveness may be needed. And these cases have, so far as I can see, almost nothing to do with defiance—either of the moral law or of some other notion of an authoritative command.

There are, alas, many acts in my own past that I can recall only with pain and some degree of self-hatred: shame that I could have been the sort of person who performed the acts for the reasons that I did and fear that the seeds of such a person might still remain within me. (I regret being autobiographical, but I do not see how one can profitably discuss these issues in the abstract.) I recall cases such as these: revealing that I was ashamed of my father in front of my college roommates and deeply hurting his feelings, betraying a school friend and shunning him because of parental pressure—a shameful act of the kind so painfully and eloquently portrayed in William Maxwell's novel *So Long, See You Tomorrow*—and, at a later stage in life, abandoning a vulnerable junior colleague in circumstances where my support was expected and needed. (J. L. Austin once queried: "How many of you keep a list of the kinds of fool you make of yourself?" Apparently, I keep such a list.) The list I have presented contains merely three (and by no means the most serious) of the many moral failures that I will never get fully out of my memory; and, if I wanted to group them under one heading, the heading would involve the *hurt* I wrongfully caused or failed to prevent—*not* some abstract notion of defying the moral law.

But wait a minute, someone might now say. Is there not an easy way to qualify Hampton's original defiance claim and make it work for the cases just presented? Is not at least one moral law the one that reads

"treat all people properly," and are not the cases that I have painfully re-
counted from my own past (cases like the ones portrayed by Wilson and
Maxwell) simply cases where I have defied *that* moral law?

I do not think that this will work. Hampton, you will recall, concep-
tualizes immorality as rebelliously defying the moral law because one
wants to satisfy one or more of one's "wishes"—by which I assume she
means some selfish aim. But in the cases I have described I was not
aware of any *defiance* or *rebellion*—what I did in these cases being too
base and weak to merit such heroic and assertive words. (Rebellious defiance seems more likely to generate pride—improper pride of
course—than guilt and shame.) In the cases described I was merely an
ordinary human bad actor; I was not Milton's Satan.

Neither was I clearly driven by the claims of what Kant calls "the
dear self." Kant tends to overestimate the role of selfishness and egoism
in explaining immorality, and I think that Hampton is tempted to follow him in this mistake. The moral failings for which I retain some self-
hatred, however, have rarely been so motivated. They have rather been
motivated by such things as weakness and thoughtlessness, the insecure
desire to fit in and not stand out in front of a peer group, flawed ideas of
such virtues as friendship and professionalism and family loyalty, mis-
placed allegiance to law and other rules, petty and ill-tempered vanity,
moral cowardice, and occasionally even outright cruelty and malice—
none of these (as Bishop Butler taught us) being selfish or mere wishes
in any ordinary sense. (Again, I am wagering that the list I have provided
is not highly idiosyncratic.)

So where are we in understanding moral hatred—self-loathing on
moral grounds? If I am right, this is often to be found in the injury we
bring to others by our wrongful treatment of them.

Do we then have a complete grasp of the kind of moral self-hatred
that seeks self-forgiveness? Not quite, I think, and I would be inclined
to add at least four additional discussions to what has been said thus far.

(1) Sometimes we may experience self-hatred where there is no responsible wrongdoing on our part at all—for example, the guilt one
might feel over being a survivor of the Holocaust or of a battle where
many of one's friends died. This, sometimes called "survivor guilt," has
been labeled as an instance of "nonmoral guilt" by Herbert Morris—
nonmoral because it does not involve culpable wrongdoing. However,
since this kind of guilt—as Morris himself points out—rests on the
morally relevant and admirable property of human solidarity, it seems
to have at least one important moral dimension. Thus when Hampton

and others claim that such guilt is simply "inappropriate," I think they are being hasty.

(2) One might also experience self-hatred in cases where one has done the right or even the morally obligatory thing. There is an old World War II movie—the title of which I have forgotten—that portrays a submarine captain (played, almost certainly, by John Wayne) who is forced to crash-dive his submarine to save it from aircraft attack—leaving a couple of his sailors on deck where they drown. He surely did, all things considered, the right thing. Even the dead sailors, if asked in some "original position," would surely have agreed to the principle of saving the ship and the majority of the crew even at the cost of a few lives. However, the captain is eaten up with guilt, self-loathing, and begins to engage in heavy drinking and other self-destructive behavior. He did not defy any moral rules—indeed he consciously acted on the moral rule that was controlling in the situation—and he did not treat anyone with a lack of respect. And yet his feelings here seem very human and understandable—and even moral to the degree that feelings of solidarity with our fellows count, as I think they do, as moral feelings. He needs self-forgiveness—something he is more likely to get from acceptance by the friends and families of the dead sailors (an acceptance that is at least very like forgiveness) than by some intellectual argument that, all things considered, he did the right thing. After all, he knows this already and still aches with self-hatred simply because he was the causal instrument of the deaths of his sailors and would not be surprised, human beings being what they are, if the friends and families of those sailors viewed him with aversion—as tainted—simply because of that instrumental connection.

Although we would surely want this captain, eventually, to overcome his self-hatred, it strikes me as a point in favor of his character that he for a time experiences such a feeling. I thus resist regarding the feeling as merely inappropriate or irrational or neurotic. (It is not, for example, like the self-hatred that is sometimes felt by totally innocent incest victims.) Strong feelings of solidarity with our fellow human beings are to be commended; but—and here is the downside—such feelings preclude one's easily avoiding all guilt and self-hatred merely by noting "It was not my fault" or even "I did the right thing." If I am correct about this, then perhaps we need to be skeptical about any simple attempt to draw a sharp contrast between moral feelings and nonmoral feelings. Perhaps even Nancy Snow's case of the football player who drops the pass merits a reconsideration.

(3) Self-hatred is sometimes felt over what might be called failures of virtue or excellence—cases where the failures have no victim except perhaps oneself. Thus a person who cannot overcome an addiction to heroin or alcohol might feel self-loathing—even if no harm comes to others—simply because of a weakness of character he regards as shameful. Although he might seek self-forgiveness, it is hard to see how he could coherently secure it through forgiveness from others—since, given that there is no other person he has wronged, there is no other person to forgive him. He might, of course, be aided in his journey toward self-forgiveness by the love or compassion of others; but not all acts of love are acts of forgiveness.

(4) Self-hatred surely admits of degrees—a point that may be obscured by the very strong language Hampton uses in her discussion. She speaks—in passages I quoted earlier—of the wrongdoer as seeing himself as "cloaked in evil," "infected with moral rot," having "nothing good or decent in him," and experiencing the "hell of self-loathing."

This language strikes me as, in most cases, excessive. The self-hatred I experienced in the cases noted earlier—though genuine and aptly, perhaps, described as self-hatred—never led me to believe that there was "nothing good or decent in me" or that I was "cloaked in evil." This language may be appropriate for the Nazi ethnic cleanser or the rapist of children but is too extreme to be applied nonneurotically to ordinary human venality. In cases where this language is literally appropriate, perhaps the persons involved really are in rebellion against morality itself and—having inflicted unforgivable wrongs—should never be forgiven by others or themselves. Perhaps, if they do not relish the lifetime of self-loathing they have earned, they should simply kill themselves. Or perhaps such persons are best left to God. I really do not know what to say about cases this extreme.

Whatever one may counsel for such moral monsters, however, it would be highly misleading in my judgment if we took the reactive attitudes appropriate to these cases of extreme evil and tried to apply them intact to the more ordinary cases. At the very least, such application would introject into our moral lives a greater degree of high drama than is typically appropriate.

So: Let us for the moment leave Nazis, persons who feel self-loathing solely because of a lack of virtue, and persons who feel survivor guilt. These cases must be mentioned in a complete survey of self-loathers seeking self-forgiveness, but they are not the cases that were of central focus in Hampton's discussion. For what she wanted, it will be recalled, was a kind of self-loathing that might properly be overcome through forgiveness by others; and the cases just discussed, for a variety of reasons, do not fall neatly into that category. My primary focus, therefore, must here be on cases where victims of wrongdoing might, by their acts of forgiveness, generate self-forgiveness in wrongdoers— such self-forgiveness being, according to Hampton, "perhaps the greatest good that forgiveness can bring."

I have up to this point been trying to identify a concept of self-hatred that could both be a legitimate target of self-forgiveness and could be accounted for on a plausible theory of immorality. I have rejected Hampton's defiance view of immorality in favor of an account of immorality as harming value incarnate in persons.

With this background, I am now—at long last—ready to move to a discussion of the other two questions I promised to explore: Under what circumstances is self-forgiveness a good? How might forgiveness from another (one's victim of earlier wrongdoing) bring about self-forgiveness? My discussion here will of necessity be very compressed and will perhaps even seem dogmatic.

Self-forgiveness strikes me as an unambiguous good only in cases where the wrongdoer has inflicted an injury for which repentance and atonement are appropriate and where that wrongdoer has in fact sincerely repented and atoned. Absent the requisite change of heart, self-forgiveness is probably hasty and is a sign of nothing more than moral shallowness.

Listen to the comfortable state to which the killer Richard Herrin brought himself after undergoing some Christian counseling about the need for self-forgiveness. After a mere three years in prison on an eight-to-twenty-five-year sentence for "heat of passion" manslaughter, Herrin thought that he had suffered enough for brutally beating his former girlfriend Bonnie Garland to death with a hammer. He is being interviewed by the psychiatrist Willard Gaylin:

HERRIN: I feel the sentence was excessive.

GAYLIN: Let's talk about that a little.

HERRIN: Well, I feel that way now and after the first years. The judge had gone overboard. . . . Considering all the factors that I feel the judge should have considered: prior history of arrest, my personality background, my capacity for productive life in society—you know, those kinds of things— I don't think he took those into consideration. He looked at the crime itself and responded to a lot of public pressure or maybe his own personal feelings. I don't know. I'm not going to accuse him of anything, but I was given the maximum sentence. This being my first arrest and considering the circumstances, I don't think I should have been given eight to twenty-five years.

GAYLIN: What do you think would have been a fair sentence?

HERRIN: Well, after a year or two in prison. I felt that was enough. . . . [Bonnie's dead] but there's nothing I can do about it. . . . She's gone—I can't bring her back. I would rather that she had survived as a complete person, but she didn't. . . . I'm not saying that I shouldn't have been punished, but the punishment I feel is excessive. I feel I have five more years to go, and I feel that's just too much. . . . I don't see any purpose in it. It's sad what happened, but its even sadder to waste another life. I feel I'm being wasted in here.

GAYLIN: . . . Are you saying two years of prison is a very serious punishment considering what you did?

HERRIN: For me, yes. (Gaylin, 1982, pp. 325–327)

Herrin's exercise in self-forgiveness has, in my view, been aptly described by Michael Moore as simply "shallow, easily obtained self-absolution for a horrible violation of another" (Moore, 1987, p. 214) Being in *this* state is surely not a good; and bringing another to this state—by an act of forgiveness or in any other way—is surely not a good thing to do. It is nice to be able to get on with one's life and not be crippled or destroyed by too much self-hatred—but only, in my view, in cases where one has earned the right to go on by appropriate repentance and atonement.

There are also, of course, different ways of going on. The fact that, after repentance, we should retain enough affection for ourselves to get on with our lives does not have to mean that we should not carry some burdens of guilt and shame—even a little bit of self-hatred—forever. These burdens may properly humble us without crippling us. It is, after all, possible to have a somewhat tragic view of human life, including one's own, without being destroyed or defeated by that view—an insight often missed in popular writings on self-forgiveness where terminally upbeat cheerfulness is the insufferable order of the day.

It should be obvious from what I have said so far that I am very skeptical about the value of forgiving wrongdoers—self or others—in the absence of sincere repentance on their parts.

Hampton says that forgiving wrongdoers may "enable [them] to forgive themselves by showing them that there is still enough decency in them to warrant renewed associations with them" (Murphy and Hampton, 1988, pp. 86–87) But how can they be shown this if it is *not true*; and how can it be true if the wrongdoer is unrepentant? If the wrongdoer is unrepentant, he generally does not (in my view) merit forgiveness. If he is already repentant, the forgiveness may be appropriate but can aid lit- tle in his moral rebirth, since, given his repentance, he is already well down the road toward moral rebirth. At most forgiveness can support and reinforce what is already there. Jean thinks that forgiving wrongdo- ers contributes greatly to both their moral rebirth and to their reaccep- tance. I think that she is right about the latter, but—for the reasons noted—I have considerable skepticism about the former.

The differences between Jean and me on this topic may be a result of the fact that she has interpreted Christian commands to forgive in a way that I do not. Many strands of Christianity—though not, as I have ar- gued earlier, all—make forgiveness unconditional—a free gift or act of grace. My own view is more cautious—perhaps even stingy. Jean, for example, does not follow me in demanding repentance as a precondi- tion of forgiveness and writes as follows:

> Even if the wrongdoer hasn't separated himself from the immoral cause, forgiving him is warranted if the forgiveness itself would effect the separation by softening his hardened heart and thus breaking his rebellion against morality. (Murphy and Hampton, 1988, p. 84)

Of course, we have all heard stories where repentance and rebirth have been generated from a free gift of forgiveness without awaiting re- pentance—the rebirth of Jean Valjean in *Les Misérables* being the most famous literary example. I would not for a moment deny the possibility of these stories. I would, however, suggest that there might be other stories that are equally or more common—stories where rebirth was generated by the desire to earn, through repentance, the thus far with- held forgiveness and love of the person victimized.

I am reminded here of the famous story of Lord Bacon, who, when he asked a priest the meaning of a large painting in a seacoast church, was told that it represented all of the sailors who had been saved from drowning through prayer. "And where," asked Bacon, "do you hang the picture of those who were not saved?" I fear that, when Hampton and others write uncritically of the redemptive power of receiving forgive- ness, they are being a bit like this priest.

Let me now bring to a close this discussion of self-forgiveness—a discussion enriched, I think, by the thought of Jean Hampton even at places where I have ultimately disagreed with her.

My main concern in this chapter has been to caution against what some have called "cheap grace"—easy self-forgiveness that is unearned and undeserved for the unrepentant wrongdoer. I believe that a certain degree of self-hatred is appropriate for people who have done grave wrongs. Indeed, if the wrong is grave enough, some degree of self-hatred should perhaps survive even sincere repentance. Should not the rapist of children, even if repentant, hate himself to some degree to the end of his days? At the very least we can surely say this: Although God may certainly forgive all such people, hasty and shallow attempts at self-forgiveness on their parts are not merely unseemly but are harmful to their own moral characters. For how is their moral rebirth to be possible if they have already decided that they are okay just the way they are?

But should we not all—as kind and generous people—have an interest in making others feel okay? ("Have a nice day!") And is not the "helping profession" of psychotherapy in particular committed to this as its primary objective?

Let me now pass directly to this topic: forgiveness in psychotherapy.

SEVEN

FORGIVENESS IN PSYCHOTHERAPHY

There is, in the contemporary world of counseling, an increasingly visible movement called "philosophical counseling"—a movement that seeks to make the discipline of philosophy more central to counseling than the discipline of psychology. Although this movement has just started to gain attention in America, it has already attained some prominence in other countries—for example, Israel, Germany, and the Netherlands. It seems that the influence of philosophy on the practice of counseling is currently of sufficient weight that even some who would not identify themselves as philosophical counselors now impose philosophical constraints on their psychological research and practice. For example, a recent essay by psychologist Robert D. Enright on forgiveness in counseling, an essay I will discuss in more detail later, explicitly makes "philosophical rationality" a condition of appropriateness in counseling.

As a professional philosopher, I greet this entry of my discipline into a new and practically important field with mixed feelings: delight that my discipline might be put to use in helping those with problems in living and fear that my discipline might be used in irresponsible ways— either by psychologists who do not understand philosophy well enough or philosophers who do not understand psychology well enough. Some careful thinking is surely in order here, and the purpose of this chapter is to make a start toward such thinking in a limited area of counseling practice: counseling forgiveness.

I should begin by noting that I am not a counselor, philosophical or otherwise, and that I have no expertise in the practice of counseling. I have become interested in this topic because my wife, who is a professional counselor, recently brought to my attention the great emphasis that forgiveness—both of self and others—now receives in counseling literature and practice. In particular she brought to my attention the work of the psychologist Robert D. Enright and his Human Development Study Group at the University of Wisconsin at Madison. Since Enright is, in effect, the "guru" of forgiveness in counseling, my remarks here will be directed in the main at his work—particularly at his influential essay "Counseling within the Forgiveness Triad: On Forgiving, Receiving Forgiveness, and Self-Forgiveness."

Before beginning my critique, however, I want to stress that I have great regard for some of Enright's writings; and some of his other writings are more cautious and nuanced than the ideas contained in the essay I will discuss. This essay is, however, typical of the forgiveness boosterism that I want to challenge—a boosterism that is currently widespread in psychological counseling, not merely among Enright's students but among many other psychotherapists. One who doubts this can, as I suggested earlier, simply visit the self-help and recovery section of a local bookstore and note the pervasiveness of messianic proforgiveness literature.

Both on my own and in collaboration with Jean Hampton, I have written on forgiveness as an issue in moral, political, and legal philosophy; and it is my hope that these studies might allow me to bring to bear a useful perspective on the role of forgiveness in another area: counseling. Since I am painfully aware that this a new area for me, and one in which I totally lack expertise, my remarks here will be extremely tentative—mainly raising questions rather than providing theories and answers of my own—and aimed primarily at generating discussion. Perhaps counselors can have their thoughts and practices about forgiveness enriched by philosophers; and perhaps philosophers can have their speculations about forgiveness enriched by learning how forgiveness works (or does not work) in a context that is generally unfamiliar to them. Or perhaps not. We will not know until we try some crossdisciplinary discussions and see how they go. This chapter is an attempt to generate one such discussion.

Before passing to the specific discussion of forgiveness and counseling, however, let me raise one general question about philosophical counseling. I assume that counseling in general has as its goal improving the lives and functionings of clients—making them more viable in the primary arenas (if Freud was right) of work and love. The ideal, I suppose, is that they should become happy—or at least, to cite Freud again, that their neurotic incapacitating anxieties should be replaced by ordinary unhappiness.

I would assume that philosophical counseling, if it is truly philosophical, will be to some degree guided not merely by such therapeutic values as anxiety reduction but also by the value that is arguably intrinsic to philosophy itself: the value of *rationality* in the realms of belief and morality. Could, for example, a philosophical counselor welcome therapeutic improvement in a client that results from that client's coming to embrace a metaphysical view that the philosopher might find irrational—even superstitious? I fear a possible dilemma here: If the intellectual merits of the comforting and therapeutic views of the client are irrelevant, then why call this form of counseling "philosophical"? If the intellectual merits are relevant, then will not the philosophical counselor at least sometimes experience a tension between the desire to support whatever will move the client toward viability and the desire to give no support to—and perhaps even to challenge—worldviews that (in the view of the philosophical counselor) cannot survive philosophical skepticism?

In his introduction to *Essays on Philosophical Counseling*, Ran Lahav suggests that philosophical counseling should avoid the "dogmatic approach" found in traditional philosophical systems. Philosophical counseling, he writes, "does not provide philosophical theories, but rather philosophical thinking tools."

Unfortunately, this claim by Lahav raises—at least for me—more questions than it solves. Most systematic philosophers have not been dogmatic in the sense of simply asserting views to be accepted as articles of faith. They have rather offered *arguments* or *reasons* for those views; and, if these are persuasive reasons, what is wrong with bringing the views to bear on counseling? If something is wrong, then one needs to argue for this and not merely hurl the insult "dogmatism." If counseling requires only the "thinking tools"—the methods of analysis and critical thinking—characteristic of philosophy, and not any of the conclusions that philosophers have reached using those methods, then how does philosophical counseling differ from the cognitive approaches (using such techniques as cognitive restructuring) that have been around in psychotherapy for a long time?

Consider an example germane to my present inquiry. Suppose a philosophical counselor believes that a particular client will never achieve his sought-after happiness or even viability unless he forgives himself. But suppose, on philosophical grounds, the same counselor is persuaded of the retributive theory of punishment and suffering—persuaded that justice demands that culpable wrongdoers suffer in proportion to their evil or iniquity. Perhaps the counselor also believes that victims have a right to have their vindictive feelings satisfied, at least to some degree, by such suffering on the part of the wrongdoer. Now finally suppose that the counselor believes that his client has done something so culpably evil that he ought to suffer for a long time—perhaps even unto death.

Would such a counselor want to lead his client toward self-forgiveness (and its potentially cleansing and restorative healing) or might he instead think (given his philosophical views, quite understandably) that this client should—absent deep repentance and atonement perhaps—*never* attain self-forgiveness but should forever suffer the self-hatred he so richly deserves?

Martin Buber (thinking perhaps of former Nazis who might seek therapeutic help?) once cautioned therapists that, in their desires to help clients overcome neurotic guilt, they should not do anything that might prevent clients from dealing properly with what he called their "authentic" or "existential" guilt. Contemporary counselors do not get too many former Nazis these days, of course, but they probably do get their share of those deep in the evil of their own existential guilt—those who, for example, physically and sexually abuse their own children. Should these children be encouraged by counselors to forgive those who have visited these unspeakable horrors on them? Should the perpetrators of those horrors be encouraged to forgive themselves? If so, is this because—in the realm of counseling—the value of client well-being gets to trump all other values? Or is it because a background worldview is being tacitly presupposed—a particular Christian perspective of love and forgiveness, perhaps—that might not withstand philosophical scrutiny or that might compromise the "do not impose your values" principle that many counselors recite as a near mantra? These are the questions to which I shall now turn.

Enright writes of what he calls "the forgiveness triad": forgiveness of others, accepting forgiveness from others, and forgiving oneself. Although I suspect that he would not refer to himself as a philosophical counselor, he appears to accept a philosophical constraint on acceptable counseling with respect to each aspect of his triad when he writes that "each aspect is . . . presented as philosophically rational and therefore appropriate within counseling. . . . We . . . make a philosophical case for [forgiveness] as both rational and moral" (Enright, 1996, p. 108).

Unfortunately, Enright does not explain what he means by "philosophical rationality." (He does find one philosopher, Margaret Holmgren, who agrees with him; but agreement with one philosopher, even as talented a philosopher as Margaret Holmgren, can hardly be a test for philosophical rationality.) Neither does Enright explain why philosophical rationality is an acceptable constraint on counseling. These two omissions are importantly related, of course, since the plausibility of the constraint will surely to some degree depend on how the operative concept in that constraint is analyzed. In addition, for reasons noted previously, even the most plausibly analyzed concept of philosophical rationality might be in tension with therapeutic goals if those goals are conceptualized in terms of making the client feel and function better by, for example, removing anxiety. Though a philosophically rational morality might acknowledge anxiety reduction as a legitimate goal, it surely would not regard it as a dominant or controlling goal. There are clearly some puzzles here that require more thought.

It is possible, of course—although Enright has provided neither an analysis of philosophical rationality (including morality) nor an argument for why such an analysis should constrain counseling—that an answer to both of these worries will emerge from the details of his discussion. Thus I shall now turn to the triad itself. Because of space limitations, I will focus mainly on forgiveness of others and treat the other two elements in the triad in a much more cursory way.

Why is forgiving those who wrong us thought to have therapeutic value? Enright is aware that some philosophers have argued that resentment of injuries may be a sign of self-respect and that therefore a too ready willingness to forgive, rather than being a virtue, may actually exhibit the vice of servility. (Enright cites Joram Graf Haber for this view, but Haber clearly gets the view from me, who, in turn, probably got it from combining the views of Joseph Butler, Peter Strawson, and Tom Hill.)

My own version of this view—as the reader is now well aware—involves the claim that victims may be harmed symbolically as well as physically by those who wrong them. Wrongdoing is in part a communicative act, an act that gives out a degrading or insulting message to the victim—the message "I count and you do not, and I may thus use you as a mere thing." Resentment of the wrongdoer is one way that a victim may evince, emotionally, that he or she does *not endorse* this degrading message; and this is how resentment may be tied to the virtue of self-respect. (A person who forgives immediately, on the other hand, may lack proper self-respect and be exhibiting the vice of servility.) This does not mean that a self-respecting person will never forgive; but it does mean that such a person might make forgiveness contingent on some change in the wrongdoer—typically repentance—that shows that the wrongdoer no longer endorses the degrading message contained in the injury.

Against this view, Enright (following Holmgren) writes as follows:

> A forgiver who knows that the act was unjust can see his or her own status as equal to the other person, regardless of the other's stance toward the offended person. In fact, resisting the act of forgiving until the offender somehow changes is giving great power to the offender. . . . An offended person who refuses to forgive until certain contingencies are met suffers twice: once in the original offense and again as he or she is obligated to retain resentment, along with its concomitant negative cognitions and perhaps even negative behaviors....To forgive, then, is to show self-respect. (Enright, 1996, p. 109)

Who is right—Murphy or Holmgren/Enright? I am inclined to say that the answer to this question is probably highly client and context dependent; and that, because of this, no universal prescription—either "Always try to forgive" or "Never try to forgive"—is justified.

Enright and Holmgren claim that a person who fails to resent *can* see their status and dignity as not lessened by such a response, and I am happy to concede that this may be so in some cases. I am not concerned to argue that one is *obligated* to feel resentment or to retain it, only that feeling and retaining such a feeling is not always wrong and is sometimes, for some people, a mark of self-respect. What I am concerned to stress is that, while a failure to resent can be consistent with proper self-respect, it sometimes is not. There are, I think, cases that should be troubling to the uncritical boosters for universal forgiveness—cases where the victim does not "see" his moral status and dignity lessened, not because the victim's self-respect is so well grounded as to be impervious to assault but because the victim had an improperly low view of his moral status and dignity in the first place.

Some people, of course, may get their self-respect from comprehensive religious views—for example, the view that each person is a precious child of God. Given that such persons have a transcendent source for their self-respect, they may be less vulnerable to attacks mounted by their fellow humans and thus less inclined to feel resentment and more inclined to move quickly to forgiveness.

But several questions must be raised here. First, is such a comprehensive view rational to believe? Second, may such a view simply be presupposed as a given by a counselor? Third, and finally, what about those who lack such a religious vision and instead get their self-respect in more normal secular ways—that is, in ways that are dependent to a nontrivial degree on how they are treated by others? (John Rawls's treatment of the social dimension of self-respect and self-esteem in part 3 of *A Theory of Justice* is magnificent.) How are people who live their mental lives in the secular, Rawlsian world to be counseled with respect to resentment and forgiveness?

As will be obvious from later chapters, I think that the topic of forgiveness is deeply enriched by a religious—indeed, specifically Christian—perspective. My point here is thus not to doubt the value of such a perspective but rather to warn against its being tacitly presupposed and perhaps even tacitly imposed on clients who do not share it or a particular therapist's version of it.

Enright seems to see only good consequences flowing from a counseling strategy that aims at encouraging victimized clients (even such badly victimized clients as incest survivors) to forgive those who have injured them. He writes that those who undergo forgiveness counseling manifest "greater gains in forgiveness, self-esteem, and hope and greater decreases in anxiety and depression" than those in a control group (Enright, 1996, p. 111).

I find this passage puzzling for several reasons. First, it seems hopelessly circular to count greater tendencies to forgive as among the gains experienced by those who are counseled to forgive. This will, of course, count as a gain only for someone who is already committed to the general excellence of forgiveness.

Second, I would like to know more what counts as a "gain in self-esteem"—a concept Enright does not analyze. Is this merely that one feels better about oneself—something that could result if one came to think that one's status as a victim is proper, as no more than one deserves—or that one has an *accurate* conception of what it is to have full worth as a free and equal rational being?

Third, and related to this, is a concern about the circumstances in which anxiety and depression reduction are to be counted as goods. What if they come about because one comes simply to accept that one's proper status in the world is that of victim and thereby stops, as the ancient Greeks used to say, "kicking against the pricks"?

In my view, slavery and oppression and victimization are made worse, not better, when people are rendered content in their victimization. The quick counsel to love, forgive, and turn the other cheek may be viewed by some as good Christian theology, but I am not at all sure that it is always good advice for counselors to give to victims. When Marx claimed that religion is the opiate of the masses, he feared that certain religious worldviews might make oppressed people compliant cooperators in their own oppression; and I fear that forgiveness might sometimes function as such an opiate as well. How many battered women, for example, have returned to their batterers for more (and perhaps fatal) abuse because some counselor, inspired perhaps by Christianity, advised them to keep trying to save the marriage out of love and forgiveness? I do not know what the answer to this question is, but I am worried that many of the boosters for universal forgiveness do not seem even to raise such issues.

Enright claims, rightly in my view, that we need to distinguish forgiveness from reconciliation. However, his talk (much) about forgiveness seems to me disproportionate to his talk (in passing) about the dangers of letting one's forgiveness nudge one toward unwise reconciliation.

So one possible consequence of premature forgiveness is that one adopts a strategy that makes one's further victimization more likely. Such a consequence would have to be counted as a negative, surely. This is a negative consequence for the victim, but I can also imagine negative consequences for the wrongdoer. What if confronting resentment gives some wrongdoers incentives to repent and reform? If this is so, then a hasty forgiveness might contribute to their further moral corruption by depriving them of this important incentive. Thus making forgiveness contingent on repentance by the wrongdoer might in part be justified, not merely by the self-respect benefits that such a strategy sometimes confers on the victim but also by the role that such a strategy might play in the rebirth of the wrongdoer.

We have all heard, and I have previously discussed, Augustine's slogan—quoted approvingly by both Holmgren and Enright—that we should "hate the sin and not the sinner." It is hard to see how the distinction between sin and sinner can even be drawn, however, so long as the sinner remains psychologically identified with his sin. However, if he breaks the identification through repentance, then the distinction may easily be drawn; and this may be another reason why a strategy of making forgiveness contingent on repentance might often be rational.

Of course, as mentioned in the previous chapter, we all know stories where rebirth has been generated from a free gift of forgiveness without awaiting repentance—the rebirth of Jean Valjean in *Les Misérables* being the most famous literary example. I would not for a moment deny these stories. I want to insist, however, that there might be *other stories* as well—stories where rebirth was generated by the desire to earn, through repentance, the forgiveness and love of the person victimized. My point, you will recall, is not to debunk the possible value of forgiveness in some (perhaps even many) counseling settings; I am rather concerned to express skepticism about it as a general counseling prescription.

I have, of course, no idea what Enright's own religious commitments are—or even if he has any. I cannot help suspecting, however, that certain Christian assumptions—perhaps acquired simply from growing up in a dominantly Christian culture—hover behind his approach to forgiveness in counseling. Again, my point is not that I oppose this perspective. My opposition is to its being tacitly—perhaps even unconsciously—adopted and applied to those who may not share it.

One Christian assumption that Enright seems to make—one that I tend to share—is that one should draw a sharp distinction between (1) forgiveness as an internal change of heart and (2) all those external behaviors required for social and personal reconciliation. I would submit, however, that this sharp distinction is nearly unintelligible within the Jewish tradition and perhaps in part explains why repentance is such an important precondition of forgiveness within that tradition. The Christian tradition tends to emphasize purity of heart as the core of the virtue of forgiveness, whereas the Jewish tradition gives primary place to the social dimension of reintegration into the covenanted community.

Enright also wants to insist, like those Christians I discussed in chapter 4, that repentance should generally *not* be a precondition for legitimate forgiveness. He claims that "resisting the act of forgiving until the offender somehow changes is giving great power to the offender" (Enright, 1996, p. 109).

But surely this is simply *not true* in all cases. If the offender greatly wants to be forgiven by me and I am not much interested in forgiving him—at least until he repents—then it seems to me that in this case the balance of power is in my favor and not in the favor of the offender. Again, my earlier point: these matters are highly client and context dependent, and any universal prescriptions should probably be met with skepticism.

To illustrate this, let me share a couple of personal recollections. The first concerns two of my former students who became my friends, two young women whose stories I will combine to hide identity. I will name the composite person Mary—a name quite different from the names of either of the people whose stories I combine. The similarities of their two stories provide evidence—as if we needed any more, alas—of the willingness of sick or evil people to prey on the vulnerable young, even their own children.

Mary once came to me—both as a friend and as someone who had thought about such matters philosophically—seeking advice on a personal problem. Her father, who had subjected her to repeated sexual abuse when she was a young girl, had recently attempted—after many years of separation—to gain reentry into her life. The father demonstrated no signs of repentance for his past iniquity but simply seemed his old arrogant self—acting as though, since Mary was his only living child, he had a right to her giving at least the appearance of a conventional father-daughter relationship with him. It seems that he was in part motivated by a desire to look normal and respectable in the eyes of a new wife and family.

Mary found this very disquieting. She had previously broken all relationships with her father—had even changed her last name so that she would not maintain even *that* relationship—and had for years felt comfortable with that rejection, with putting the father and all he stood for utterly out of her life.

Mary's problem was this: Her minister, and several of her friends from church, kept counseling her that she had a duty to forgive the father and to welcome him back into family life—at least on limited terms. This was starting to make Mary feel both guilty and afraid—guilty because she hated going against the teachings of her religion and afraid that, if she did not continue to shun her father, the adaptive strategy that had worked so well for so long would collapse and she would suffer psychological damage.

In short, for her own well-being, Mary wanted to maintain her strategy of resentment and rejection but wanted to do so only if the strategy could be *validated*, conceptualized as rationally and morally and religiously acceptable—in contrast to having it conceptualized as sinful and un-Christian.

We had several conversations, and she read some of my writings on forgiveness and resentment—writings where I argue for the legitimacy of resentment and for making forgiveness generally contingent on repentance. As a result of these encounters, Mary claimed—with what accuracy I do not know—that I had helped her to accept the legitimacy of her continued resentments. She decided to go against her minister and retain a posture of rejection and resentment toward her father. She seemed comfortable with this—still does—

and indeed claims that the only time she was ever uncomfortable about the strategy was when her minister was trying to make her feel guilty about it.

In my more cynical moments I am inclined to suspect that her visits to me merely illustrate Sartre's claim that we seek advice from people who are inclined to tell us what we already want to hear.

To the degree that I did influence her ultimate decision, however, the case raises for me some interesting questions: Is there any reason to think that Mary's strategy of resentment and rejection was—*for her*—irrational, immoral, or untherapeutic? Was she lucky that she talked to me—was I, without realizing it, providing her with a kind of philosophical counseling?—or would it have been better had she listened to her minister and perhaps obtained counseling from an Enright disciple? What would Enright himself say about cases like this—that they do not occur (and that my understanding of this case is necessarily superficial) or that they occur so infrequently that counseling forgiveness is still the best general strategy? I do not pretend to know the answer to these questions, but I do think that they are worth asking.

Perhaps, as Enright claims, we are "often healed" when we bestow forgiveness as a free, unconditional gift. But the skeptical voice within me wants to say: "Perhaps *often not*, as well."

This brings me to my second story, one told to me by a colleague whose mother had survived the Holocaust, during which she had been personally tortured by Doctor Joseph Mengele in one of his many cruel medical experiments. This woman, now to all appearances a psychologically viable human being, was once asked by her son—my colleague—what she would want him to do if, after all these years, he ever encountered Mengele. His mother thought for a moment and simply said: "Kill him."

Is it obvious that this woman has missed out on something important—philosophically, morally, or psychologically—in never attaining a posture of forgiveness toward her torturer? If so this needs careful argument and not merely hopeful assumption.

I will not be able to discuss in any depth Enright's treatment of the final two items of his "forgiveness triad": receiving forgiveness and self-forgiveness. The ideal case of receiving forgiveness, according to Enright, involves a change in attitude and behavior—remorse, respect for the offended person, and a willingness to make amends.

So long as this does not involve imposing oneself on an unreceptive potential forgiver—for example, by making amends in an improper way or at an improper time—I see little to quarrel with in what Enright says here.

I must confess, however, that I have grown a bit tired of receiving unwelcome and time-consuming apologies from people (often former students) in various twelve-step programs—people, often totally unremembered by me, who seem to believe that they have done me some injury in the past for which they must atone. I generally let them go on with it because they are so very earnest and it seems so very important to them, but I also generally feel trapped and start to develop some resentful feelings of my own about being dragged into somebody else's agenda.

Of course, if one does decide to express forgiveness, one must do this with some care if the wrongdoer is to receive it in the proper way. Being forgiven in a spirit of arrogance or condescension is not true forgiveness, and one might properly resent it rather than accept it. Being truly forgiven as an act of love, however, might well be a step in the moral rebirth of some people (the Jean Valjean example), and Enright is instructive and persuasive in describing the details of how such a forgiveness interaction might be structured. Recall that my doubts about the universal validity of his prescription do not entail doubts about its value for a wide variety of clients in a wide variety of contexts.

I am less happy with what Enright says about self-forgiveness. In self-forgiveness, he argues, the wrongdoer moves from a position of self-estrangement to being comfortable with himself in the world. He can finally, in the vernacular, get on with his life.

But, as I argued in the previous chaper, I am not at all sure that it is morally proper for all wrongdoers to get on with their lives in this way. Returning to Buber's worries about authentic guilt, we might well wonder if certain persons—by their horrible acts—have not forfeited forever their right to be "comfortable" with themselves.

Of course, most ordinary wrongdoers, after most acts of ordinary wrongdoing, clearly have a right (after proper repentance, at any rate) to resume their lives with some if not total affection for themselves.

But what about the nonordinary wrongdoer?—the torturer, the ethnic cleanser, the abuser of children? Might we not want to say of such a person what Cynthia Ozick said of a repentant Nazi murderer—"Let him go to hell. Sooner the fly to God than he"—or what Elie Wiesel said in his prayer at Auschwitz—"God of forgiveness, do not forgive those who created this place. God of mercy, have no mercy on those who killed here Jewish children"? If we believe in the reality of evil—and do not want to excuse all wrongdoers as themselves totally

helpless victims of their own terrible childhoods and mental patholo-
gies—might we not want to say of those involved in certain evils that
they should be *brought to self-hatred*, not freed from it, and forever view
themselves as persons who have made of their lives excrement?

This hard moral vision—one that takes the past very seriously and
makes some of its evil irrevocable in human terms—probably cannot be
demonstrated as rationally superior to all competing visions; but I do
think that it has to be acknowledged as at least a respectable candidate
for a philosophically acceptable moral worldview. The upbeat vision of
ultimate trust and love that seems to lie behind much of the literature of
forgiveness is not the only viable candidate.

What bearing might the harsher moralistic view have on the practice
of counseling? Must a counselor reject the view entirely? (Are persons
who hold the view simply ill suited to be counselors?) If the counselor
does hold the view, should he or she refuse to take on persons perceived
as evil as clients? (Imagine yourself a counselor called on to help Adolph
Eichmann find peace with himself before his death. Would you accept
him as a client? Would you accept the serial rapists and the abusers and
murderers of children? Would you accept those who brutalize the eld-
erly?) If counselors do take on such clients, might they justify the practice in terms of some doctrine of role responsibility? Might they see
their role responsibility as limited simply to serving their clients rather
than considering large moral and social issues—much as a criminal defense lawyer might, in defending a dangerous criminal, seek moral insu-
lation in the role responsibility of a lawyer? Just as the lawyer might believe that matters of guilt are best left to a jury, even a counselor who
believes in evil and the retribution that evil people deserve might feel
fallible in making such determinations and believe that they are best
made by others—God perhaps—and thus might take on *all* clients in a
spirit of moral humility. Is such a posture of caution and moral humility
the proper one for a counselor to adopt, or is it merely a rationalization
that allows the counselor to avoid giving evil its due and taking responsibility for a failure to confront it?

I have raised many questions here, and I do not pretend to know the
correct answers to them. I do, however, believe that these questions
must be faced if counseling—and the role that forgiveness might play in
counseling—is to be placed in a genuine philosophical context. Such a
context will often reveal complexity and tension—a war of competing
values—and force us to see that many gains carry with them some nontrivial losses. There might even be a general tension between counseling (as client centered) and philosophy (as truth/rationality centered)—

or at least a tension between counseling and global moral concerns. If this is so, then it is better to bring this to full consciousness than to pretend that all is well so long as we practice love and forgiveness. What the Chicago School has taught us about economics may also be true for forgiveness counseling: there is no free lunch.

In his closing argument in the Loeb and Leopold sentencing hearing, Clarence Darrow made a passionate plea for the overcoming of hate by love and quoted these famous lines from Omar Khayyam: "So I be written in the Book of Love, I do not care that book above, erase my name or write it as you will, so I be written in the Book of Love."

If we could only be written in one book, then I suppose that all of us would prefer to be written in the Book of Love rather than in the Book of Resentment. Forgiveness, as an outgrowth of love, is often a wonderful—even blessed—thing; and thus I have no quarrel with those who would advocate its power and value in counseling or in a variety of other contexts. Perhaps it is even reasonable to regard it as the default position. My only concern is that allegiance to this value should not be blind—that it should be tempered with a consideration of the possibility that, for some people in some contexts, it might not be the course to be recommended by either good philosophy or good counseling.

EIGHT

FORGIVENESS AND CHRISTIANITY

I have up to this point discussed forgiveness mainly in secular terms—in terms of values that can easily be embraced by secular readers even if those values have their origin at least partially in religious traditions.

I will now move to an explicit discussion of religion and explore how a religious perspective might influence one's views on forgiveness. What difference might one's religious beliefs make to one's views on forgiveness? Since I am only an amateur in the study of both religion and theology, I am not the ideal person to seek an answer to this question. However, I am going to have a stab at it anyway.

There are, of course, many different religions and thus many different religious perspectives on forgiveness; and limitations of both space and my own knowledge make it impossible for me to pursue more than one of them here. I will, therefore, generally limit myself to certain aspects of my own religious tradition: Christianity—the only religion about which I have more than superficial knowledge.

I do not apologize for this approach—and for two reasons. First, I am very doubtful that there is any such thing as a "religious perspective" that is not a perspective tied to some *particular* religion, and one who would try to talk too generally here risks breaking ties with traditions of deep and intelligent discussion and replacing them with the shallow slogans of New Age "spirituality."

Second, even many non-Christians are inclined to agree that Christianity has made forgiveness more central than any other religious tradition. For that reason, it might be expected that this tradition would have a rich—perhaps the richest—discussion of the topic.

Even if almost everyone would agree to the centrality of forgiveness in Christian ethics and its role in understanding love of neighbor, however, not all—not even all Christians—see Christian forgiveness in the same way. For example, as I discussed earlier, some interpret Christianity as requiring unconditional forgiveness and others interpret it in such a way that repentance may be required for legitimate forgiveness. The interpretation that one adopts may, as I argued in the previous chapter, have serious and potentially harmful consequences in such contexts as psychotherapy. So even the interpretation I will offer of Christian forgiveness cannot avoid being controversial even among Christians.

I will begin by exploring some central Christian teachings about vengeance and forgiveness that can, in large measure, be accepted in secular terms—accepted even by a nonbeliever. I will then explore some Christian teachings that can be accepted only in the context of Christian commitment.

Consider, in addition to the parable of the unforgiving servant already discussed, these two passages from the New Testament: Romans 12:19, "Vengeance is mine; I will repay, saith the Lord," and John 8:7, "He that is without sin among you, let him first cast a stone at her." Both passages suggest that we humans may be too limited to be reliable seekers of vengeance. We may not *know enough* to seek vengeance with accuracy, or we may not be *good enough* to seek vengeance without hypocrisy. Both passages suggest that vengeance-seeking may reveal an unvirtuous lack of humility on our parts—a failure to see how finite and fallible we actually are. This lack of humility can make us quite dangerous—a thought no doubt in Nietzsche's mind when he warned that we should "mistrust all in whom the impulse to punish is powerful."

The passage from Romans suggests that God approves of vengeance—indeed claims it for himself (and thus must regard it as not inherently immoral)—but believes that his creatures are too fallible to be entrusted with the task. One dramatic human fallibility is cognitive: a lack of relevant knowledge.

And what is the knowledge that we humans are supposed to lack? I would say it is this: a knowledge of what I will call *deep character*. If we are to punish at all—and I see no reason to think that God thinks that all human punishment is wrong—we must be able to have reasonably reliable knowledge of such things as wrongful conduct and the mental states that are generally conceptualized as *mens rea* (intention, for example). The seeking of vengeance, however, is often driven by more than the beliefs necessary for any system of crime control. It is often driven by the belief that the person by whom one has been harmed is rotten to the core—evil all the way down—and thus a legitimate target of *hatred*. But do we really know enough about any fellow human beings to be confident that they are so fully evil, and so fully responsible for their evil, that they are legitimate objects of hatred—a hatred that seeks to take delight in their suffering? In the movies, *yes* (one reason why we can so enjoy revenge films), but in real life *probably not*. Human beings are complex concrete individuals, not cartoon or fictional characters of whom (with the help of the artist) we can have a God's-eye view. To think we can have such a view of actual people, moreover, is to live in a world of dangerous fantasy—a world that, as Nietzsche warned, may start with a expressed desire to give other people their just deserts but may end in our simply finding self-deceptive excuses for being cruel.

The writer William Trevor said this of the serial killer who is the central character of his novel *Felicia's Journey*: "Lost within a man who murdered was a soul like any other soul, purity itself it surely once had been." If one takes this perspective on another human being—no matter what that person has done—then hatred for that person becomes difficult if not impossible. With the abandonment of hatred comes the abandonment of any ability to take delight in that person's suffering. And in the absence of that delight—actual or anticipated—revenge is useless, and vindictiveness is, at the end of the day, indeed without a point.

But suppose we did not have the cognitive limitations just noted. Suppose we were in a position to have reliable knowledge of the depth of evil and responsibility and desert present in another. This would remove the epistemological problem noted in Rom. 12:19, but the problem of John 8:7 would remain: Perhaps we are ourselves too filled with inadequacy—or even evil—to seek revenge against others without hypocrisy. Suppose we follow Jesus and examine the state of our own souls—our own sinful natures—before giving in to our vindictive impulses and casting the stones of revenge. If we do this—so Jesus seems to assume—we will be overwhelmed by our own moral inadequacies and drop our stones.

Not so, claims Michael Moore in his well-known essay "The Moral Worth of Retribution." Moore ridicules Jesus' caution as "pretty clumsy moral philosophy" and dismisses its relevance when he writes:

It is true that all of us are guilty of some immoralities, probably on a daily basis. Yet for most people reading this essay, the immoralities in question are things like manipulating others unfairly; not

caring deeply enough about another's suffering; not being charitable for the limitations of others; convenient lies, and so forth.
Few of us have raped and murdered a woman, drowned her three
small children, and felt no remorse about it. (Moore, 1987, p. 188)

Moore's point seems to be this: In the relevant sense most of us *are*
without sin, and so we might as well feel free to pick up some stones and
cast away.

Is this an adequate answer to Jesus? I think not. The response is too
shallow, for it fails to reflect the kind of serious moral introspection that
Jesus is attempting to provoke. The point is not to deny that many people lead lives that are both legally and morally correct. The point is
rather to force such people to face honestly the question of *why* they
have lived in such a way. Is it (as they would no doubt like to think) because their inner characters manifest true integrity and are thus morally
superior to those people whose behavior has been less exemplary? Or is
it, at least in part, a matter of what John Rawls has called "luck on the
natural and social lottery"?

Perhaps, as even the retributivist Kant suggests in his *Religion Within
the Limits of Reason Alone*, their favored upbringing and social circumstances, or the fact that they have never been placed in situations where
they have been similarly tempted, or simply their fear of being found
out has had considerably more to do with their compliance with the
rules of law and morality than they would like to admit. Perhaps if they
imagined themselves possessed of Gyges' ring (a ring that, in the myth
in book 2 of Plato's *Republic*, makes its wearer invisible), they might, if
honest with themselves, have to admit that they would probably use the
ring, not to perform anonymous acts of charity, but to perform some
acts of considerable evil—acts comparable, perhaps, to the acts for
which they often seek the punishment of others. If they follow through
honestly on this process of self-examination, they will have discovered
the potential for evil within themselves and will have learned an important lesson in moral humility.

The lessons in human limitations found in the foregoing scriptural
passages could, of course, be embraced even by a totally secular person. Although the Christian insights serve to reinforce these facts
about human fallibility, even an atheist could grant the value of those
insights.

This is not the case, however, with all Christian teachings having a
bearing on forgiveness; and I will now, drawing in part on the insights
of the theologian Marilyn Adams, explore four such teachings that will

be found acceptable only within the context of actual Christian commitments. These Christian commitments should make one more open to forgiveness than those without such commitments.

1. *We are commanded by God to forgive our enemies and those who wrong us.* When (in Matthew 18:22) Jesus is asked how many times we should forgive, he answers "seventy times seven"—which is, I assume, a way of saying "without end." In Luke, as previously noted, this demand is attached only to the *repentant* wrongdoer.

One surely cannot be a sincere Christian and not respond "with fear and trembling" to the duties that flow from divine commands. This response is fear based, but it is not to be understood as fear of an unvirtuously slavish nature. As Peter Geach has argued, a fear of the Being who is the very ground of my own being—the one who creates and sustains me—is not like fearing Hitler or some other thug and can, indeed, be a part of love and respect.

2. *Christianity, in its stress on the fallen nature of humanity, introduces a humbling perspective on one's self and one's personal concerns—attempting to counter our natural tendencies of pride and narcissistic self-importance.* According to this perspective, we are all deeply sinful and stand in constant need of forgiveness—not just from other fellow humans but primarily from God. This perspective does not seek to trivialize the wrongs that we suffer, but it does seek to blunt our very human tendency to magnify those wrongs out of all reasonable proportion—the tendency to see ourselves as morally pure while seeing those who wrong us as evil incarnate and the failure to see that no injury we suffer can be said to be totally undeserved. By breaking down a sharp us-them dichotomy, and by revealing our own suffering, even at the hands of others, as something considerably less than a cosmic injustice (one lesson of Job), such a view should make it easier to follow Auden's counsel to "love your crooked neighbor with your crooked heart."

3. *All human beings—even those guilty of terrible wrongs—are to be seen as children of God, created in his image, and thus as precious.* This vision is beautifully expressed by the writer William Trevor in the previously quoted passage from his novel *Felicia's Journey*, when he speaks with compassion and forgiveness even of the serial killer who is the central character of that novel and writes of him: "Lost within a man who murdered, there was a soul like any other soul, purity itself it surely once had been." Viewing the wrongdoer in this way—as the child he once was—should make it difficult to hate him with the kind of abandon that would make forgiveness of him utterly impossible. It has been said that God loves even Satan because he loves all that he has created.

Seeing ourselves as precious children of God may also make forgiveness of wrongdoing easier. Why? Because it may provide a basis for our own self-respect that is less vulnerable to mistreatment from others.

4. *Finally, Christianity teaches that the universe—for all its evil and hardship—is ultimately benign, created and sustained by a loving God and to be met with hope and trust rather than despair.* On this view, the world may be falling, but—as Rilke wrote—"there is One who holds this falling with infinite softness in his hands."

Like most Christians, I find it very difficult, at least on most days of the week, to embrace such a view of the universe with a full heart—emotionally as well as intellectually. The world simply presents too much visible evidence against this view—something that has provoked theologians from the Middle Ages to today to worry about the problem of evil. However, as Kierkegaard reminds us, Christian belief is supposed to be difficult. This is why it requires faith.

To the degree that I can embrace the benign view of the universe, however, then I will not so easily think that the struggle against evil—even evil done to me—is my task alone, all up to me. If I think that I alone can and must make things right, then I risk taking on a kind of self-importance that makes forgiveness of others difficult if not impossible. Given a certain kind of faith, however, I can relax a bit the clinch-fisted anger and resentment with which I try to sustain my self-respect and hold my world together all alone.

I opened this book with a rather bleak quotation from Fay Weldon on the dangers of forgiveness—a perspective I value. In this chapter, however, I have suggested that the bleak perspective is not the only perspective and have offered a more hopeful vision—a sermon if you want to call it that—that expresses this hopeful vision.

Since the gloomy sermon involved a gloomy text, it seems only fitting that the hopeful sermon should be attached to a hopeful text. In this spirit, I offer the following from Seamus Heaney's poem *The Cure at Troy:*

> Human beings suffer.
> They torture one another.
> They get hurt and get hard.
> No poem or play or song
> Can fully right a wrong
> Inflicted and endured.
>
> The innocent in gaols
> Beat on their bars together.

A hunger-striker's father
Stands in the graveyard dumb.
The police widow in veils
Faints at the funeral home.

History says, *Don't hope*
On this side of the grave.
But then, once in a lifetime
The longed-for tidal wave
Of justice can rise up.
And hope and history rhyme.
So hope for a great sea-change
On the far side of revenge.
Believe that a further shore
Is reachable from here.

   The Cure at Troy, ll. 1–22

NINE

CHRISTIANITY AND
CRIMINAL PUNISHMENT

I could easily have ended this book with the previous chapter. For when that chapter ended, I had accomplished what I had essentially promised at the outset: To render at least plausible my belief that vindictiveness and vengeance possess some positive value, to defend forgiveness in such a way as not utterly to deny that value, to explore how repentance opens the door for legitimate forgiveness, to provide a critical examination of self-forgiveness, to illustrate how all these issues play out in the real-world contexts of criminal law and psychotherapy, and, finally, to explore the way in which a religious—specifically Christian—perspective might affect (positively or negatively, make your own judgment) one's thinking about everything previously discussed.

I have decided, however, to add this final chapter—a chapter in which I will explore the issue of criminal punishment in more detail than has been possible in the earlier chapters.

Why do I propose to do this, since this is a book on forgiveness and since I have already argued that, on most accounts of the justification of punishment, forgiveness is compatible with demanding punishment?

My rationale for this chapter is that it is very commonly believed that forgiveness—particularly Christian-based forgiveness—is incompatible with, perhaps all punishment and, certainly, with such extreme punishments as the death penalty. Given that this is commonly believed, and given that I think that the belief is mistaken, I think it is worth trying—in some detail—to get clear on the matter.

As one seeks to get clear, however, one will come to see—I think—
that the mistaken belief is not wildly mistaken; that indeed it poses an
important challenge to the practice of punishment. The challenge is
this: Even if the command to forgive does not directly preclude punishment, does not the more basic command from which even the command to forgive flows preclude punishment? What command is this?
The command that we are to *love*—both God and our neighbor. This is
the issue I will now explore: To what degree, if at all, is the Christian
love commandment consistent with criminal punishment?

I suppose that some of my readers may at this point be wondering
why they should even care about this issue. Why is it important to try to
understand Christianity on punishment?

The answer to this question is, I assume, obvious to those who are
Christians, since Christians are surely committed to viewing all important issues in terms of the best interpretations of their faith; and many
of them will also seek to have some of their views enacted as a matter
of public policy—unless, of course, they have been argued (wrongly,
in my view) into submission by their readings of such philosophers as
John Rawls (Murphy, 2001).

There are at least three reasons why even non-Christians should find
the issue of interest, however. First, the Christian tradition—along with
certain other religious traditions—is one of great spiritual, moral, and
intellectual power. As such it surely contains wisdom that can be appreciated by those of other faiths and even by those who are agnostic or
atheist. As I have argued earlier with respect to forgiveness, for example,
the parables of Jesus contain many insightful nuggets that can be mined
partly for secular purposes.

Second, some of the greatest philosophical minds that have addressed
the topic of punishment were deeply influenced by Christianity. One
thinks of such obvious examples as Augustine, Aquinas, and Kant.

Third, the Christian tradition, for better or for worse, has been and
remains (at least in rhetoric) highly influential in the moral outlooks of
a great many people in a variety of countries—an influence that surely
affects the politics of such issues as capital punishment. This is certainly true in the United States, for example, where people on both
sides of the capital punishment debate often use biblical references in
order to claim the moral high ground. Such references sometimes
even appear in remarks of lawyers and judges in actual criminal cases.
Whatever one may think of the ultimate legitimacy of such references, it is surely worth attempting to understand a tradition that has
such great influence.

In seeking to develop a Christian framework for the understanding of criminal punishment—or indeed for any other evaluative issue—a controlling value will surely be that of *love*. The coming of Christ is explained in scripture as a result of God's love of the world, and the imitation of Christ tradition has made love central. Paul famously identified love as the greatest of the Christian virtues (1 Corinthians 13). Writing centuries later on capital punishment, the theologian Bernard Häring puts it this way: "It would not be in harmony with the unique fullness of salvation and its loving kindness to apply drastic [Old Testament] directives without any qualification as obligatory in the present order of salvation and grace" (Häring, 1966, p. 124).

Not all Christians, of course, would find Häring's claim worthy of full endorsement. It is interesting to note in this regard that some of the most prominent contemporary Christian defenses of capital punishment tend to come from the fundamentalist religious right and that they draw heavily and mainly on the very Old Testament teachings that Häring wishes to blunt and qualify. These fundamentalists presumably do not reject the centrality of a gospel of love but rather see no inconsistency between that gospel and the harsh Old Testament teachings.

I shall here thus simply assume that the centrality of love in the Christian perspective can be granted. The difficulty, of course, is in developing the proper interpretation of that value and how it is properly to be applied in the domain of punishment.

The value of love may initially seem not only different from but at odds with the value of *justice* that is normally thought to control legitimate thinking about the law and particularly at odds with the harsh treatment that is often demanded under the heading of just punishment. This is not, however, a conclusion to which one should jump in haste. Indeed William Temple, former archbishop of Canterbury, argued that justice, properly understood, is a part of love, properly understood. Lord Denning quotes him as claiming, "It is axiomatic that love should be the predominant Christian impulse and that the primary form of love in social organization is justice" (Denning, 1997, p. 3).

In trying to think coherently about the relation between Christian love, justice, and law, we should try to resist a hasty tendency among some secular liberals to embrace a liberal and sentimental vision of Christianity and then to chide actual Christians for their hypocrisy in not living up to that vision. This tendency is revealed on the topic of punishment—particularly capital punishment—when Christians who support the death penalty may be condemned, without even hearing their reasons, as not really Christian at all. "How can you claim that love of neighbor is the primary value," it may be asked, "and then support the death penalty—the most unloving response to another human being that can be imagined?" Even some Christians argue in this way, of course—for example, in a recent essay on capital punishment, Garry Wills suggests that if President Bush would read his "favorite philosopher" (Jesus) more carefully he would not support the death penalty.

This way of attempting to put Christians on the defensive may involve a variety of mistakes and confusions. First, it is important to note that the initial and primary part of the love commandment is that Christians are to love *God*. Jesus—reinforcing the Jewish law as taught in Deuteronomy (6:5) and Leviticus (19:18)—endorses this formulation of the command: "You shall love the Lord your God with all your heart, and with all your soul, and with all your strength, and with all your mind; and your neighbor as yourself." (Luke, 10:25) Seen in this context, love of one's neighbor must surely be constrained by—and in part explained by—the love of God. Thus if there is reason to think that God would command or find permissible the punishment of wrongdoers even with death—and herein lies the possible relevance of Old Testament passages—then such punishment cannot so easily be dismissed as unloving in the most relevant sense.

Christian love, in other words, is not simply a matter of being nice and cuddly—of giving everyone a warm hug, saying "Have a nice day," and then sending them on their way. Recall in this regard Jesus whipping the money changers in the temple (John 2:14), moved by his righteous anger to inflict punitive violence on wrongdoers. (This scene is powerfully captured in the El Greco painting that is reproduced on the jacket of this book.) In spite of what the secular mind and even some Christians might wish, the full doctrine of Christian love is to be found not simply in the films of Frank Capra but also in the grim stories of Flannery O'Connor and in the hard and demanding theologies of Augustine and Kierkegaard. "God loves you—whether you like it or not," as the bumper sticker says.

A second point worth noting is that, for the Christian, what happens to the human soul—in this life and the next—is of primary concern. (Note that the love commandment is endorsed by Jesus as the correct answer to the question "What must I do to inherit eternal life?") Thus a central concern for the Christian with respect to punishment must be not simply what will happen to the body in this life but what will happen to the soul eternally; and those who are impatient with such a worry must of necessity be impatient with Christianity at its core and thus with much of what Christianity will have to say about punishment.

Physical death, on the Christian view, is not the end of the person and is not the gravest of evils we can imagine or inflict. Physical death is the beginning of a process that can end either in what *is* the gravest of evils—eternal estrangement from God—or the greatest of goods, eternal communion with God. Jesus puts it this way: "Fear not them which kill the body, but are not able to kill the soul: but rather fear him which is able to destroy both soul and body" (Matthew 10:28).

The Christian punishment debate thus cannot ignore, and must indeed emphasize, this question: What effect will punishments of a certain sort have on the soul of the person being punished and on the souls of other members of the community? (If you are more comfortable with secular language that is less metaphysically controversial, you may for the present substitute the word "character" for the word "soul.") If the penalty of death, for example, harms the soul of the person being punished and corrupts the souls of the law abiding, this will be a powerful Christian argument against it. If, on the other hand, the penalty of death does not have these effects—and perhaps even can plausibly be argued to benefit the soul—then something important is being said in favor of the punishment. Indeed even love, on a certain understanding, could provide a justification for it.

There will be those, of course, who will argue that harsh punishment of a person—and particularly execution—cannot possibly be of benefit to the soul or character of that person. Hurting people has the tendency to harden rather than soften their hearts, and execution faces some special problems in the realm of character reformation. In the film *My Little Chickadee*, Cuthbert J. Twillie (played by W. C. Fields) is about to be hanged and is asked if he has anything to say about his execution. He replies: "It's going to be a great lesson to me." We laugh because we sense some absurdity in the idea that a person can be taught something and thus improved by his very extinction.

But our laughter—if uncritical—may be a bit hasty here; for we also tend to laugh at Dr. Johnson's observation: "Depend upon it, Sir, when a man knows he is to be hanged in a fortnight, it concentrates his mind wonderfully." Here we laugh, not at absurdity but at the surprising realization that he might be on to something important. The prospect of death can, after all, provoke soul-searching, repentance, and open the door to salvation—an intentional theme of Tolstoy's *Death of Ivan Ilych* and a perhaps unintentional theme of the Tim Robbins film *Dead Man Walking*, a theme that to some degree undercuts the film's attempt to be a sermon against the death penalty. The repentance and spiritual rebirth of the Sean Penn character is the single most impressive thing in the film, and one wonders if this would ever have happened had he not been facing execution.

My point so far has simply been to argue that the relationship between Christianity and criminal punishment—even the death penalty—may be much more complex than it initially appears to some. It is not to be understood in terms of a few simple clichés about love, mercy, and forgiveness and may indeed emerge as an issue on which Christians may find themselves in great tension.

This tension is dramatically revealed in Kant's writings on punishment. Kant is famous for his defense of retributive punishment and sometimes defends punishment, particularly capital punishment, with an enthusiasm that many regard as unseemly. At other times, however—particularly when he is explicitly writing as a Christian—he provides arguments that raise doubts about such punishment. He thus reveals the kind of instructive ambivalence on the issue that is also found in such other important Christian thinkers as Augustine.

Both Augustine and Kant regard our actual world as fallen and sinful—a world in which even those seeking to promote justice and order and even love will risk having their efforts corrupted by the evil and depravity latent in their own natures. Absent the belief in ultimate grace and salvation, this worldview may properly be called *tragic*; for it condemns even the best of human efforts, such as the rule of law, to the very corruptions those efforts seek to oppose. We always risk doing evil even when we use punishment to restrain evil. As Nietzsche put it, there is always a danger that in doing battle with monsters we become monsters. The Earthly City can never, through human effort alone, become the City of God.

If Christian love is not simply being nice—even very, very nice—then what is it? In a recent essay, Thomas J. Shaffer suggests that such love, at least in the social and political sphere, is to be analyzed in terms of *forgiveness*. He speaks of "the politics of forgiveness" and "a community constituted by forgiveness" and seeks to develop what he calls a "jurisprudence of forgiveness." Influenced mainly by the writings of the late theologian John Howard Yoder, Shaffer sees most current law as unnecessarily coercive and even violent—claiming that the Christian religion is fundamentally at odds with the law on the matter of forgiveness. He makes his point most dramatically in the following passage concerning those securely imprisoned on death row:

> There is no rational argument any longer to kill them—much less the common good argument Caiaphas had for killing Jesus. Legal

power, it seems, has to kill them anyway, if only because it would not be legal power if it didn't. Law here cannot take the risk of forgiveness. Forgiveness would remove the fear, the accountability, and the responsibility that law provides—and thus, as law sees it, would invite chaos. . . . [F]orgiveness disrupts legal order. (Shaffer, 2001, pp. 325–326)

I learned a great deal from Shaffer's essay, and I certainly share one view that he emphasizes: one very important way in which Christian love would have to address the issue of crime and punishment is through concern for the poor and the otherwise disadvantaged and the willingness to make significant sacrifices to alleviate their sufferings. This is why I closed my chapter on repentance with a discussion of collective repentance in the context of crime and punishment. ("As you have done it unto one of the least of these my brethren ye have done it unto me"; Matthew 25:40.)

However, Shaffer's tendency to see law—and particularly legal punishment—as necessarily at odds with forgiveness strikes me as confused and thus quite mistaken. There is no doubt that some of our present penal practices are at odds not only with Christian forgiveness but with any civilized notions of moral decency, but this fact is insufficient, in my view, to support a wholesale indictment of law and punishment.

The main reason why I want to reject Shaffer's claimed conflict between law (especially legal punishment) and forgiveness should by now be obvious to the reader. On my view, following Bishop Butler, forgiveness is mainly a matter of a change of heart—not external practice.

So can forgiveness of a person, so understood, then be compatible with the continued demand that the person be punished—perhaps even executed? In my view the answer to this question is yes. It all depends on the *motive* or *reason* for the demand. If the motive or reason is to express hatred, then—of course—there is immediate inconsistency; for, if one still hates, then one has not forgiven. Thus an appeal to Christian forgiveness does constitute a powerful attack on legal punishment to the degree that such punishment is driven by hatred. Of course, if one is doing something truly horrendous to another human being, the chance that hatred and cruelty are behind it should not be too quickly dismissed; and many present penal practices in America are, alas, hard to understand on any other terms.

Perhaps callous indifference also deserves a place next to hatred as something Christians should guard against in the realm of punishment. Recall again the parable of the unforgiving servant. The sin of the servant in inflicting harsh treatment on his own servant was not, presumably, based on any hatred he had for the servant. It was rather a total indifference to the adverse life circumstances that caused the servant to become indebted and to fear harsh punishment for failing to pay the debt—the very kind of life circumstances that the master had taken account of when he showed mercy to the unforgiving servant for the nonpayment of his own debt.

Suppose, however, that the motive or reason for punishment is not grounded in hatred or some other evil passion. Suppose rather that it is grounded in the sincere belief that punishment of this nature is necessary to control crime and thereby promote the common good or that it is required by justice. Then there is no inconsistency. Thus these two passages from Kant, which on the surface may strike many people as inconsistent, seem to me not inconsistent at all:

From *Rechtslehre* (*The Doctrine of Right*):

Even if a civil society were to dissolve itself by common agreement of all its members . . . the last murderer remaining in prison must first be executed, so that everyone will duly receive what his actions are worth [in proportion to their inner viciousness] and so that the bloodguilt thereof will not be fixed on the people . . . as accomplices in a public violation of legal justice. (Kant, 1996, p. 474)

From *Tugendlehre* (*The Doctrine of Virtue*):

It is . . . a duty of virtue not only to refrain from repaying another's enmity with hatred out of mere revenge but also never even to call upon the world-judge for vengeance—partly because a man has enough guilt of his own to be greatly in need of forgiveness and partly, indeed especially, because no punishment, no matter from whom it comes, may be inflicted out of hatred. . . . Hence men have a duty to cultivate a *conciliatory spirit*. But this must not be confused with *placid toleration* of injuries, renunciation of the rigorous means for preventing the recurrence of injuries by other men. (Kant, 1996, p. 578)

Kant's point—a point that would, I think, be embraced as quite orthodox by most Christians—is that love does not forbid punishment. What it forbids is *punishment out of hatred*. What Jesus and Paul counseled (Matthew 25:42–46; Hebrews 13:3), it will be recalled, is that we visit and comfort those in jail; they did not counsel the abolition of jails. To visit and comfort those in jail or prison—even those justly there—is a way of saying that they are still loved and not hated: that their essential humanity is still being acknowledged. Such love is quite consistent, however, with thinking that they deserve to be there and that society benefits from their being there.

Of course, the possibilities of self-deception here are enormous— particularly the possibility that, as Nietzsche warned, we use the rhetoric of justice and the common good in order to hide from ourselves the fact that our actual motives are spite, malice, envy, and cruelty—what Nietzsche called *ressentiment*. Thus emphasizing forgiveness may be an important corrective to what we are actually doing in contrast to what we say and even consciously think we are doing.

It is also important to remember, however, that self-deception also poses dangers in the realm of leniency—that the self-satisfactions of being kind and showing mercy to the criminal before us may blind us to the fact that such kindness may be very unkind to others to whom this criminal poses a danger and thus may not be, all things considered, a genuine act of Christian love after all. Kant makes this point when, in his *Rechtslehre*, he expresses skepticism about pardons—a skepticism that former President Clinton's casual awarding of pardons has, alas, given us all reason to share. The point is also well expressed by Angelo in Shakespeare's *Measure for Measure* when—illustrating that even deeply flawed people can sometimes have great insight—he says:

> I show [pity] most of all when I show justice,
> For then I pity those I do not know,
> Which a dismissed offense would after gall;
> And do him right that, answering one foul wrong,
> Lives not to act another.
>
> (Act 2 , scene 2)

The issue of self-deception in our understanding of punishment is very important, and I will return to it later.

If the argument that I have sketched here is correct, then it is correct to say that Christian love and Christian forgiveness are both quite compatible with the advocacy and infliction of punishment. This does not entail, however, that these Christian virtues are compatible with punishment *whatever the purpose of the punishment* or *whatever the nature of the punishment*.

What should the Christian say about the purposes of punishment and about the range of permissible punishments? I have already noted that punishment based in hatred—punishment the purpose of which is merely to satisfy the hatreds felt by victims and the law-abiding—may be ruled out. Thus, if all the currently trendy psychobabble about punishment as giving victims something called "closure" means satisfying victim hatred, then Christians may on religious grounds be opposed to such victim satisfaction.

I say "may" instead of "must" here, however, since I think that the issue of victim satisfaction is very complex. Remember that the great eighteenth-century moral philosopher and Anglican bishop Joseph Butler, while preaching at Rolls Chapel in London, delivered a powerful sermon, "Upon Resentment," in which he noted both the universality and the legitimacy (within limits) of resentment toward wrongdoers. Surely, Butler reasoned, a loving God would not have implanted such a passion in his creatures if it did not have some useful purpose; and he argued that the useful purpose is *defense*—defense of the moral and legal order. True allegiance to morality and law is not merely intellectual but also must be revealed in passionate commitment; and indignation and resentment (a kind of self-referential indignation) represent such commitment.

So if resentment can be distinguished from hatred (and again the temptations of self-deception here are enormous), then satisfying victim resentment might consistently be a part of a Christian account of punishment. Unlike hatred, resentment may evince a legitimate concern with the validation of the victim's social worth. Of course, Christians, like all fair-minded people, will worry about the equality concerns I raised in my earlier discussion of victim impact statements as ways of institutionalizing even justified resentment.

On the issue of the nature of punishment, I think that it is reasonably safe to say that Christians (along with all other decent people) would want to rule out punishments administered in an arbitrary and capricious (e.g., racist) way and, of course, rule out brutally inhumane punishments and brutally inhumane treatment of criminals. All this is surely inconsistent with Christian love as generally understood. Thus such punishments as torture and mutilation and the practice of putting prisoners at grave risk of rape should presumably be opposed by Christians.

Suppose we now have at least a rough idea of what is ruled out. What is left in? Is *retribution*, for example, a legitimate purpose of punishment? Is *capital punishment* legitimate? These are the issues to which I shall now turn.

Augustine and Aquinas regarded promotion of the common good to be the primary value that gives secular punishment its legitimacy. The value of living lives that are happy and meaningful in purely human terms has never been denied by any except the most puritanical of Christians, and social order is clearly required for such happiness. In addition, such religious values as salvation may be made harder to make the focus of one's attention when one is at risk of being tormented by assorted outlaws and thugs—those whom it is the business of the criminal law and its mechanism of punishment to restrain. Even Kant, most famous for the retributive elements in his theory, recognized the importance of such teleological considerations in his account of punishment. Recall in the passage quoted earlier from the *Tugendlehre* that Kant warns against letting a charitable disposition encourage a laxity in law enforcement that will constitute "renunciation of the rigorous means . . . for preventing recurrence of injuries by other men."

In addition to the promotion of the common good, Christians will also presumably unite around any punishments that work meaningfully toward the spiritual transformation of the criminal—a theme pursued in my earlier chapter on repentance and the law.

The barbarism that is all too common in the pestholes that many American prisons—and particularly jails—are can hardly be imagined to have such an effect, but we can envision changes in the system— changes of a kind that have been richly discussed by Antony Duff, for example, and explored in an earlier chapter. Faith-based prison programs—though constitutionally problematic in the United States—also seem to have some success in this regard, although much of the evidence for this success remains anecdotal.

On both of these issues—promotion of the common good and character reformation—a Christian evaluation will, like all teleological evaluations, be highly dependent on reliable empirical evidence with respect to the actual consequences of our punitive practices.

But what about retribution? Is it a legitimate objective on a Christian view of punishment? In his recent essay, "Catholicism and Capital Punishment," Avery Cardinal Dulles—giving the orthodox Catholic position originally articulated by Augustine and Aquinas—lists retribution as one of the legitimate common good objectives of criminal punishment.

Is he right about this? This depends, I think, on just what one means by "retribution." In the philosophical literature on punishment, retributive punishment is usually understood as giving the criminal what he, in justice, *deserves*. There are, however, at least six different accounts of what might be meant by "desert" and thus at least six different versions of retributivism: desert as legal guilt; desert as involving *mens rea* (e.g., intention, knowledge); desert as involving responsibility (capacity to conform one's conduct to the rules); desert as a debt owed to annul wrongful gains from unfair free riding (a view developed by Herbert Morris); desert as what the wrongdoer owes to vindicate the social worth of the victim (a view developed by Jean Hampton); and, finally, desert as involving ultimate character—evil or wickedness in some deep sense (what Kant calls "inner viciousness")—a view that I find present in Michael Moore's essay, already mentioned, "The Moral Worth of Retribution."

Section 2266 of the most recent edition of the *Catechism of the Catholic Church* claims that "redressing the disorder introduced by the offense" is the "primary aim" of punishment. This seems to incorporate elements of the views found in Morris and Hampton and is probably what Cardinal Dulles means by "retribution."

It seems to me that there is no inconsistency between the essentials of Christianity and the first five forms of retributivism noted. With respect to the sixth, however—what I will call "deep character retributivism"— there does seem to me an inconsistency. Thus this strikes me as a form of retributivism that Christians should oppose, and I doubt that Cardinal Dulles would disagree. Relevant here are the insights contained in scriptural passages, two already noted: "Vengeance is mine, saith the Lord" (Romans 12:19), "Let him who is without sin among you cast the first stone at her" (John 8:7), and "Judge not that ye be not judged" (Matthew 7:1). Presumably what is being ruled out here is not *all* judgments of value—unless one wishes to follow the lead of *The Living Bible*, a frequent source of unintended humor, which renders the passage as "Don't criticize, and then you won't be criticized." What is rather being ruled out, I think, are ultimate judgments concerning deep character. "The Lord does not see as mortals see; they look on the outward appearance, but the Lord looks on the heart" (1 Samuel 16:1–13).

I have earlier argued that judging the very soul of another human being and attempting to decide his ultimate desert is beyond the scope of human ability and must be viewed as a task either to be left undone or reserved for God. Human beings simply do not *know enough* to make such judgments with accuracy. In addition, human beings are simply not *good enough* to make such judgments without hypocrisy. These are the main points, in my view, of the noted scriptural passages.

There is, of course, a puzzle here: If we do not know enough to punish for inner viciousness, how can we know enough to tell if various methods of punishment advance or retard the improvement of the soul? How can the inner self be opaque to us in one context but not in the other? And can even *mens rea* be saved if such skeptical worries are taken seriously? The classic philosophical problem of other minds may here raise its ugly head.

My own hunch—which I can only sketch here—is that this problem grows in seriousness the greater the depth of inquiry into the inner life—for example, I suspect that judgments of intention (and other *mens rea* judgments) are more reliable and safer than judgments of inner viciousness, judgments that a person is hopelessly rotten to the core. They are safer in part because they do not to nearly the same degree tempt us to cruelty and to dismissing the very human worth of the wrongdoer. It is, I think, easier to retain one's loving virtue in ascribing a particular intention to a person than it is in ascribing to that person a "wanton, hardened, abandoned, and malignant heart"—to use some language that has appeared in the law of homicide and in capital sentencing.

Perhaps skepticism about deep character retributivism also involves worries about *responsibility* and not only worries about knowledge and goodness. Except for the famous remark about "inner viciousness" quoted earlier, Kant is generally skeptical of attempts to use secular punishment to aim at what I have called deep character retributivism. Kant's retributivism, except for that one remark, is better explicated in terms of the ideas of paying a debt and restoring a moral balance.

Kant's skepticism about deep character retributivism—a skepticism particularly vivid in his explicitly religious writings—involves worries about ultimate responsibility. Though this is a great oversimplification, we can sometimes witness in these religious writings the Pelagian Kant's transformation into an Augustinian Kant. In the famous moral writings (e.g., *Grundlegung*), Kant subscribes to a doctrine of radical freedom and responsibility. In *Religion*, however, he seems to accept what John Hare has called "the moral gap"—the gap between our knowing what we ought to do and our ability to do it. In his *Religion Within the Limits of Reason Alone*, Kant claims that this gap can be bridged only with the aid of what he calls "an inscrutable outside power"—that is, the grace of God. To the degree that Kant subscribes to this Augustinian view, he provides additional reasons for rejecting deep character retributivism—reasons raising skeptical doubts about ultimate responsibility that supplement the skeptical doubts about knowledge and goodness that have already been mentioned.

Whenever we presume to condemn deep character, self-deception again poses a problem, because—as Socrates noted long ago—there are few things we human beings more enjoy than thinking that we know more than we do. To this can be added the narcissistic joys of thinking that we are better than we are or that we are more in control than we are. Seeing criminals as two-dimensional cartoon monsters, instead of as fellow human sufferers, is one way this self-deception reveals itself. Although it is not common to use the word "eloquent" with respect to Kant's prose, the most eloquent exposure I know of this kind of self-deception occurs not in Nietzsche but in Kant's *Religion*. He writes:

> A man's [inner dispositions of character], sometimes even his own, are not observable; and consequently the judgment that the agent is an evil man cannot be made with certainty. . . . [People] may picture themselves as meritorious, feeling themselves guilty of no such offenses as they see others burdened with; [but they never inquire] whether good luck should have the credit, or whether by reason of the cast of mind . . . of their own inmost nature, they would not have practiced similar vices had not inability, temperament, training, and circumstances of time and place which serve to tempt one . . . kept them out of the way of these vices. This dishonesty, by which we humbug ourselves and which thwarts the establishing of a true moral disposition in us, extends outwardly to falsehood and deception of others. If this is not to be termed wickedness, it at least deserves the name worthlessness, and is an element in the radical evil of human nature . . . that constitutes the foul taint of our race. (Kant, 1960, p. 33)

Of course, if inner wickedness is to some degree opaque to us, then so too will be inner goodness; and if we should not judge a person for his deep character viciousness, then it may not be consistent to praise and reward him for (for example) his repentance. As Montaigne reminds us in his essay "Of Repentance," "These men make us believe that they feel great regret and remorse, but of amendment and correction or interruption they show us no sign. . . . I know of no quality so easy to counterfeit as piety."

I wonder if the Christian could avoid the inconsistency by arguing in this way: Mistakes with respect to judgments of goodness are generally less worrisome and dangerous than mistakes with respect to judgments of deep character evil. (So what if Mother Teresa turns out not to have been—at her core—as grand as we thought when we were singing her praises.) Most of us probably do think that it is unjust to hand out praise and prizes to those who are less than fully deserving—but not nearly as grave an injustice as administering blame, humiliation, and suffering to those who do not deserve it. Whatever the wrong of thinking that people are better than they in fact are, it at least does not involve *giving up* on them. And it is giving up on people—coming to think that they are unworthy of any attempt at human community with them—that is perhaps the consequence most to be feared from judgments of inner wickedness. And do we want to allow the state—which cannot even deliver the mail efficiently—to act on its hunches about inner wickedness and the punishment that such wickedness deserves?

What about capital punishment? Is its advocacy consistent with Christianity properly understood? Of course, the fact that so many prominent Christian philosophers and theologians have been supporters of capital punishment should make one pause before hastily assuming that the practice is un-Christian. However, the enthusiasm expressed by these thinkers for capital punishment has often been radically overstated by supporters of the death penalty. The radio show host and newspaper columnist Dennis Prager, for example, has cited Augustine as a Christian authority to support his belief in the legitimacy of capital punishment. He quoted this passage from *The City of God*: "It is in no way contrary to the commandment 'thou shalt not kill' to put criminals to death according to law or the rule of natural justice."

Augustine did indeed make this claim, but it takes a great deal of creative free association to turn this into a statement of support for the death penalty. And getting Augustine right is a matter of some importance, since—after Jesus and Paul—he has probably done more than anyone else to create what might be called "the moral tone" of Christianity.

I read Augustine—and I here impose on him a modern distinction he might not have welcomed—as asserting the *right* of the state to execute but also arguing that it is almost always *wrong for the state to exercise that right*. The state may not be denied to have, in the abstract, the right to execute if this promotes the common good or promotes personal salvation. However, one can hold this view and also consistently hold that, in every particular case one knows of, that execution does not in fact promote these goals—the only goals that would justify it. Augustine frequently argues in just this way and indeed, for all his reputation to the contrary, offers some of the most eloquent objections to capital punishment ever given in our culture.

In a letter to Marcellinus, the special delegate of the Emperor Honorius to settle the dispute between Catholics and Donatists, Augustine is concerned with the punishment to be administered for what must have, to him, seemed the most vicious of crimes: the murder of one Catholic priest and the mutilation of another by members of a radical Donatist faction. He wrote:

I have been a prey to the deepest anxiety for fear your Highness
might perhaps decree that they be sentenced to the utmost
penalty of the law, by suffering a punishment in proportion to
their deeds. Therefore, in this letter, I beg you by the faith which
you have in Christ and by the mercy of the same Lord Christ, not
to do this, not to let it be done under any circumstances. For although we [bishops] can refuse to be held responsible for the
death of men who were not manifestly presented for trial on
charge of ours, but on the indictment of officers whose duty it is
to safeguard the public peace, we yet do not wish that the martyr-
dom of the servants of God should be avenged by similar suffering, as if by way of retaliation. . . . We do not object to wicked
men being deprived of their freedom to do wrong, but we wish it
to go just that far, so that, without losing their life or being
maimed in any part of their body, they may be restrained by the
law from their mad frenzy, guided into the way of peace and san-
ity, and assigned to some useful work to replace their criminal activities. It is true, this is called a penalty, but who can fail to see
that it should be called a benefit rather than a chastisement when
violence and cruelty are held in check, but the remedy of repentance is not withheld? (quoted in Burt, 1999, pp. 195–196)

This is just one of many similar passages to be found in Augustine's
sermons and letters—passages that, at the very least, should make supporters of the death penalty stop counting him as among their Christian
boosters.

The Protestant Kant was, of course, an enthusiastic supporter of
capital punishment; and even if his Christianity made him generally
skeptical of using secular punishment to target inner viciousness, it
never seemed to make him skeptical of the death penalty itself. It can be
argued, however, that if Kant had correctly applied his own moral theory he would have opposed the death penalty. Such an argument was
developed, for example, by Hermann Cohen—a leading figure among
the Marburg neo-Kantians.

Let me now draw this somewhat rambling free association on Christianity and punishment to a close. I have suggested that there cannot be
anything that might reasonably be called *the* Christian view on punishment. Christianity is compatible with a variety of different views, even
about capital punishment.

I do think, however, that it can be said that certain considerations
must be regarded as central to any Christian approach to punishment—

considerations that should be taken seriously by all Christians, even if all Christians (perhaps in part because they read the empirical evidence differently) do not agree on the exact weight to be given to the various considerations. By way of summary and conclusion, I will briefly identify five, as follows.

1. Punishment must be consistent with the primary value of love—which means, at the very least, that punishments based in hatred must be opposed. Christians will emphasize the virtue of forgiveness as a means of overcoming such hatred.

2. Punishment is best justified in terms of promotion of the common good and the spiritual reformation of the criminal. This second goal, as interpreted by Christians, would surely be rejected as illegitimate by such neutrality liberals as Ronald Dworkin. The Christian, of course, should seek the best evidence available on whether particular punishments actually accomplish these goals or are only said to accomplish them by those who prefer to think about these matters in a shallow way. Only by such careful attention to relevant evidence can one transcend anecdotes and steer between the Scylla of excessive and cruel harshness and the Charybdis of excessive and sentimental leniency.

3. To the degree that retribution is a legitimate goal of criminal punishment, one must not presume that in giving the criminal the punishment that he deserves one is giving him the suffering that is appropriately proportional to the inner wickedness of his character. If human beings have the proper degree of moral humility, they will see that punishment on these grounds must be left to God. If they lack that humility, they will simply confirm Nietzsche's observation that we should mistrust all persons in whom the urge to punish is strong.

4. Punishment will never be pursued with righteous enthusiasm but always with caution, regret, and humility—with a vivid realization that we are involved in a fallible and finite human institution that is, even if necessary, regrettable. That it may be a necessary evil does not stop it from being an evil. Christians, believing that even the best of human endeavor is tainted with human depravity, should be on the watch for self-deception and realize, with Nietzsche, that all the high-sounding human talk about justice and desert and the common good often serves simply as a mask for cruelty.

5. Many Christians, without hypocrisy or inconsistency, will be disinclined to defend an absolute prohibition against capital punishment. These Christians will not, for example, tend to see capital punishment as an evil comparable to the intentional killing of the innocent—something that most Christians will surely regard as absolutely wrong in

principle. They will, however, be extremely cautious about supporting capital punishment—nervous about turning over the guilty/innocent distinction to the secular state and seeing capital punishment, with Augustine, only as an absolutely last resort, justified perhaps in the abstract but very rarely, if ever, justified in fact.

This Augustinian view is central in the new final paragraph on capital punishment in the most recent edition of *The Catechism of the Catholic Church*. The paragraph draws its authority from the 1995 encyclical *Evangelium Vitae*:

> Today . . . as a consequence of the possibilities which the state has for effectively preventing crime, by rendering one who has committed an offence incapable of doing harm—without definitively taking away from him the possibility of redeeming himself—the cases in which the execution of the offender is an absolute necessity "are very rare, if not practically nonexistent." (Section 2267)

Christians will always be alert to the fact that, from a Christian point of view, there is no more serious way of harming a person than to pose obstacles to that person's opportunity to repent, reform, atone, and thereby open himself to the possibility of redemption and salvation. Hamlet, you will recall, did not want to kill Claudius at prayer because he wanted to send Claudius to hell and thought that, if he killed him in a state of grace, this would not happen. Hamlet's desire was, of course, deeply sinful; and the modern death penalty, while presumably not aiming at the eternal damnation of the criminal, may show an indifference to the possibility of such damnation that a Christian would find troubling. Of course there is Dr. Johnson's observation about the prospect of being hanged focusing the mind, but one would surely want to have more than amusing anecdotal evidence for this before letting it form the basis for justifying execution.

In short: If there is good reason to believe that execution generally stands in the way of repentance and rebirth of the criminal or if there is good reason to believe that such punishment generally reinforces cruelty and other sinful dispositions in the law-abiding or if there is no compelling reason to think that capital punishment is required for the common good, then Christians will presumably oppose capital punishment. My own view is in accord with the position taken in the *Catechism of the Catholic Church*—namely, that the case against capital punishment on these grounds is very strong.

I know that there is theological controversy over the degree to which Old Testament doctrine is incorporated into Christianity and the degree to which Christianity transcends that doctrine. This is a controversy into which I am incompetent to enter. However, I am reasonably confident that most Christians would want to endorse—and give high priority to—these words of Ezekiel: "I have no pleasure in the death of the wicked; but that the wicked should turn from his way and live" (32: 11).

CONCLUDING REMARKS

[Those who] preach "cheap grace" . . . fail to see what it means for the gospel to call men and women to the cross, to intensify their darkness before driving it away.

Rowan Williams, Archbishop of Canterbury

As this book has progressed, it has—like my own life—moved with increasing sympathy toward forgiveness and toward a religious framework for thinking about forgiveness and related issues.

Even at my most sympathetic attachment to forgiveness, however, I have tried to retain a sense of the legitimacy of resentment and other vindictive passions. They are deeply encoded and—within limits—highly useful passions, for they can be instruments of our self-defense, our self-respect, and our respect for the demands of morality.

Because of the value of the vindictive passions, their overcoming in forgiveness must be seen as a risky business. For in hasty forgiveness we risk weakening or even losing some of our strategies of defense. We also risk supporting a morally flabby worldview wherein wrongdoing is not taken seriously and in which wrongdoers are given insufficient incentives to repent, atone, and repair.

Of course, even the most sympathetic writings on forgiveness tend to recognize that forgiveness is *hard*—a difficult thing to accomplish. They see this difficulty mainly in psychological terms, however—that is, the difficulty always present when one attempts to control strong passions. In this way the difficulty of forgiving is seen as on a par with the difficulty of controlling a bad temper, controlling compulsive behavior, or controlling such evil passions as malice or racial hatred.

In contrast to this, I tend to see the difficulty more in *moral* terms—the difficulty of knowing how far one can go in the direction of forgiveness without compromising *values of genuine importance.*

In this way, the difficulty bears some analogy to Luther's famous remark "Here I stand. I can do no other." In making this claim, Luther was surely not saying that he was finding himself physically or psychologically compelled to do what he did. (He was not suggesting that his foot was nailed to the floor or that he had a strange psychological compulsion to post notices on doors.) Rather he was saying that, given his own weighing of competing values, his moral and religious sense forced him to conclude that the course of action he was taking was morally and religiously required of him. And in making that choice, he surely felt that something of value was being left behind. This is why he struggled and saw his choice as in many ways a dilemma.

So, too, with forgiveness. One who adopts this as a strategy sets sail on a risky sea—seeming less risky, no doubt, if one believes that the universe and one's own value are sustained by a loving God, but risky none the less. This is because the choice between genuine values, unlike the choice between clear goodness and clear evil or the choice between reason and compulsion, opens the door to the possibility of serious and perhaps even irrevocable mistakes.

A main part of the message of this book has been that the choice between forgiveness and vindictiveness is not a choice between reason and compulsion. Those who see the choice in these ways miss, in my view, not only the dangers of forgiveness (the dangers of vindictiveness are obvious) but also the nature of the struggle to attain forgiveness. They thereby distort and cheapen the value of what has been attained.

It has also been my concern in this book to argue that muddled sentimental thinking about forgiveness can have serious consequences in such otherwise diverse areas as criminal law and psychotherapy.

In the area of criminal law, hasty sermons about love and forgiveness can make us lose sight of the genuine values served by systems of punishment. These values include not merely the obvious values of protection against crime but also the value of treating most (but of course not all) wrongdoers with the dignity that attaches to their being viewed as responsible agents who deserve the moral compliment of being resented and even punished. I certainly want my own wrongdoing to be viewed in this way and would feel insulted and degraded if others viewed me merely as pitiful, sick, and myself as much a victim as those whom I have wronged. Do I not thus owe other wrongdoers at least the initial presumption that they, too, are legitimate objects of blame, resentment, and punishment?

In the realm of psychotherapy, hasty and uncritical leaps to forgiveness may cause some people (victims of abuse for example) to let down their guards and open themselves to further abuse—to accept as necessary a victim status that they ought instead to resist both emotionally and behaviorally. To the degree that resentment and other vindictive passions are a part of such a strategy of resistance, then—unless they run to excess—these passions should be welcomed.

In summary, I think that the main message of this book has been this: Even as we rightly preach the virtues of forgiveness, we should recognize that victims deserve to have their vindictive passions respected and to some degree validated. Even if these passions should not be the last word, they have a legitimate claim to be the first word. Even when they should not control, they should be listened to with respect instead of met with pious sermons and sentimental, dismissive clichés.

We may grant that the vindictive passions represent a darkness within us that we hope ultimately to drive away. This darkness sometimes gives a bit of initial relief, however, as it partially shields us from the painfully intrusive light cast into our souls when we are deeply wronged by our fellow human beings—a light that shatters our innocence by illuminating our fragility, our vulnerability, our openness to suffering and betrayal.

FURTHER READING

The Case for Forgiveness

Those seeking a strong and often persuasive advocate for forgiveness will find one in the writings of Robert D. Enright—called by *Time* magazine "the forgiveness trailblazer." I suggest these four:

Robert D. Enright, "Counseling Within the Forgiveness Triad: On Forgiving, Receiving Forgiveness, and Self-Forgiveness," *Counseling and Values 40, 2*, January, 1996.

Robert D. Enright and Joanna North, eds., *Exploring Forgiveness* (with a foreword by Bishop Desmond Tutu)(Madison: University of Wisconsin Press, 1998).

Robert D. Enright and Richard P. Fitzgibbons, *Helping Clients Forgive* (Washington, DC: American Psychological Association, 2000).

Robert D. Enright, *Forgiveness Is a Choice* (Washington, DC: American Psychological Association, 2001).

Other Books That Make a Case for Forgiveness

Trudy Govier, *Forgiveness and Revenge* (London: Routledge, 2002).

Michael E. McCullough, Kenneth I. Pargament, and Carl E. Thoresen, eds., *Forgiveness: Theory, Research, and Practice* (New York: Guilford, 2000).

Some Cautions About Forgiveness

Sharon Lamb and Jeffrie G. Murphy, eds., *Before Forgiving: Cautionary Views on Forgiveness and Psychotherapy* (New York: Oxford University Press, 2002).

The Case for Resentment, Vindictiveness, and Revenge

Jean Améry, "Resentments" in his *At the Mind's Limits* (New York: Schocken Books, 1986). An Auschwitz survivor, Améry explores—with extraordinary self-awareness and honesty—the complex resentments he directs toward prosperous and self-confident post-war Germany. He closes his essay with a question he cannot answer: "I must encapsulate my resentments. I can still believe in their moral value and their historical validity. Still, but how much longer?"

Peter A. French, *The Virtues of Vengeance* (Lawrence: University Press of Kansas, 2001). Peter is my colleague at Arizona State University. I sometimes fear that the presence on the same campus of two people with so much to say in favor of vindictiveness—me with two cheers, Peter with perhaps three—will confirm the belief of many that Arizona still operates with an Old West mentality.

Susan Jacoby, *Wild Justice: The Evolution of Revenge* (New York: Harper, 1983).

Robert Solomon, "Justice v. Vengeance—On Law and the Satisfaction of Emotion," in *The Passions of Law*, edited by Susan Bandes (New York: New York University Press, 1999).

Responding to Global Evil and Mass Violence

Martha Minow, *Between Vengeance and Forgiveness: Facing History After Genocide and Mass Violence* (Boston: Beacon Press, 1998). The Govier book noted above also has useful things to say on these issues.

Works That Have Particularly Influenced My Thinking

Marilyn Adams, "Forgiveness: A Christian Model," *Faith and Philosophy 8*, 1991. This essay criticizes some of my early work on forgiveness and caused me to view with much greater sympathy the Christian perspective on forgiveness.

Joseph Butler, *Fifteen Sermons Preached at the Rolls Chapel* (especially Sermon VIII—"Upon Resentment"—and Sermon IX—"Upon Forgiveness of Injuries"). These sermons were first published in 1726. Unfortunately, there is no complete edition currently in print. However, they are usually easy to find in libraries and (I have been told) a complete edition will soon appear from Liberty Press.

Thomas E. Hill, Jr., "Servility and Self Respect," *Monist 57*, January, 1973. One moral philosopher who has greatly influenced my thinking is Immanuel Kant. Tom Hill is one of the most distinguished contemporary philosophical commentators on Kant, and his essay on servility and self-respect pursues a Kantian analysis in language of far, far greater clarity than Kant's own.

Aurel Kolnai, "Forgiveness," *Proceedings of the Aristotelian Society 74*, 1973-74.
Peter Strawson, "Freedom and Resentment," *Proceedings of the British Academy*, 1962. Reprinted in *Freedom and Resentment and Other Essays* (London: Methuen, 1974).
P. Twambley, "Mercy and Forgiveness," *Analysis 36*, 1976.
Simon Wiesenthal, *The Sunflower*, Revised and Expanded Edition (New York: Schocken Books, 1997). Wiesenthal tells the story of a dying Nazi who asks a Jewish prisoner to forgive him for the atrocities in which the Nazi participated. This powerful story—raising many deep questions—is followed by brief essays from various writers (philosophers, theologians, novelists, etc.) who address in different ways the question "Should the Jewish prisoner offer forgiveness to this person in these circumstances?"

Some of My Own Publications Relevant to the Present Topic

"Forgiveness and Resentment," *Midwest Studies in Philosophy 7*, 1982.
Forgiveness and Mercy (co-authored with Jean Hampton. Murphy: Chapters 1, 3, 5; Hampton: Chapters 2 and 4) (Cambridge: Cambridge University Press, 1988).
"Repentance, Punishment, and Mercy," in *Repentance*, edited by Amitai Etzioni (Lanham, MD: Rowman and Littlefield, 1998).
"Jean Hampton on Immorality, Self-Hatred, and Self-Forgiveness," *Philosophical Studies 89*, 1998.
"Moral Epistemology, the Retributive Emotions, and the 'Clumsy Moral Philosophy' of Jesus Christ" in *The Passions of Law*, edited by Susan Bandes (New York: New York University Press, 1999).
"Two Cheers for Vindictiveness," *Punishment and Society 2*(2), April 2000.
"Shame Creeps Through Guilt and Feels Like Retribution," *Law and Philosophy 18*, 1999.
"Forgiveness, Reconciliation, and Responding to Evil," *Fordham Urban Law Journal 27*, June 2000.
"Religious Conviction and Political Advocacy," *The Modern Schoolman 78*, January/March 2001.
"Christianity and Criminal Intent," *Punishment and Society 5*(3), July 2003.

Other Works and Authors Noted

Adams, Robert M., *Finite and Infinite Goods* (New York: Oxford University Press, 1999).
Aeschylus, *Oresteia*, translated by Robert Fagles (New York: Viking, 1975).
Aristotle, *Nichomachean Ethics*, translated by Robert Crisp (Cambridge: Cambridge University Press, 2000).
Auden, W. H., "As I Walked Out One Evening," in *Collected Poems* (New York: Vintage, 1991).

Augustine, *The City of God*, translated by Henry Bettenson (New York: Penguin, 1984). Useful quotations from Augustine's other works—including the letter to Marcellinus that I quoted in my final chapter—may be found in Donald X. Burt, *Friendship and Society: An Introduction to Augustine's Practical Philosophy* (Grand Rapids, MI: Eerdmans, 1999).

Buber, Martin, "Guilt and Guilt Feelings," in his *The Knowledge of Man* (New York: Harper and Row, 1965).

Broad, Charlie Dunbar, *Five Types of Ethical Theory* (London: Routledge and Kegan Paul, 1930).

Coetzee, J. M., *Disgrace* (New York: Viking, 1999).

Denning, Lord, *The Influence of Religion on Law* (Canada: Canadian Institute for Law, Theology, and Public Policy, 1997).

Doctorow, E. L., *Ragtime* (New York: Random House, 1975).

Duff, R. A., *Trials and Punishments* (Cambridge: Cambridge University Press, 1986).

Duff, R. A., *Punishment, Communication, and Community* (New York: Oxford University Press, 2001).

Dulles, Avery Cardinal, "Catholicism and Capital Punishment," *First Things*, April, 2001.

Fingarette, Herbert, "Punishment and Suffering," *Proceedings of the American Philosophical Association 50*, 1977.

Gaylin, Willard, *The Killing of Bonnie Garland* (New York: Simon and Schuster, 1982).

Geach, Peter, *God and the Soul* (London: Routledge and Kegan Paul, 1969).

Haber, Joram Graf, *Forgiveness* (Lanham, MD: Rowman and Littlefield, 1991).

Hampton, Jean, "The Moral Education Theory of Punishment," *Philosophy and Public Affairs 13*, 1984.

Hampton, Jean, "The Nature of Immorality," *Social Philosophy and Policy 7*(1), 1989.

Hampton, Jean, "Mens Rea," *Social Philosophy and Policy 7*(2), 1990.

Hampton, Jean, "Correcting Harms Versus Righting Wrongs: The Goal of Retribution," *UCLA Law Review 39*, 1992.

Hare, John E., "Augustine, Kant, and the Moral Gap," in *The Augustinian Tradition*, edited by Gareth B. Matthews (Berkeley: University of California Press, 1999).

Häring, Bernard, *The Law of Christ*, Volume 3 (Westminister, MD: The Newman Press, 1966.)

Heaney, Seamus, *The Cure at Troy* (New York: Noonday Press, 1991). This is a performing version of Sophocles's play *Philoctetes*.

Hijeulos, Oscar, *Mr. Ives' Christmas* (New York: Harper Collins, 1995).

Holmgren, Margaret, "Forgiveness and the Intrinsic Value of Persons," *American Philosophical Quarterly 30*, 1993.

Horney, Karen, "The Value of Vindictiveness," *American Journal of Psychoanalysis 8*, 1948.

Irving, John, *The Hotel New Hampshire* (New York: Dutton, 1982).

Kant, Immanuel, *Metaphysical First Principles of Right* (*Rechtslehre*), *Metaphysical First Principles of Virtue* (*Tugendlehre*), and *Groundwork of the Metaphysics of Morals* (*Grundlegung*), translated by Mary J. Gregor in *Kant's Practical Philosophy* (Cambridge: Cambridge University Press, 1996).

Kant, Immanuel, *Religion Within the Limits of Reason Alone*, translated by T. M. Greene and H. H. Hudson (New York: Harper and Row, 1960).

Kierkegaard, Søren, *A Kierkegaard Anthology*, edited by Robert Bretall (Princeton: Princeton University Press, 1946).

Kierkegaard, Søren, *Purity of Heart is to Will One Thing*, translated by Douglas V. Steere (New York: Harper and Row, 1948).

Kleist, Heinrich von, "Michael Kohlhaas," in *The Marquise of O and Other Stories*, translated by David Luke (New York: Penguin, 1978).

Lahav, Ran and Tillmanns, Maria da Venza, eds., *Essays on Philosophical Counseling* (Lanham, MD: University Press of America, 1995).

Maxwell, William, *So Long, See You Tomorrow* (New York: Vintage, 1996).

Montaigne, Michel de, *The Complete Essays*, translated by Donald Frame (Palo Alto, CA: Stanford University Press, 1958).

Moore, Michael, "The Moral Worth of Retribution," in *Responsibility, Character, and the Emotions*, edited by Ferdinand Schoeman (Cambridge: Cambridge University Press, 1987).

Morris, Herbert, "Persons and Punishment," in *On Guilt and Innocence* (Berkeley: University of California Press, 1976).

Morris, Herbert, "A Paternalistic Theory of Punishment," *American Philosophical Quarterly 18*, October, 1981.

Morris, Herbert, "Nonmoral Guilt," in *Responsibility, Character, and the Emotions*, edited by Ferdinand Schoeman (Cambridge: Cambridge University Press, 1976).

Neu, Jerome, *A Tear Is an Intellectual Thing* (New York: Oxford University Press, 2000).

Nietzsche, Friedrich, *Beyond Good and Evil*, translated by Walter Kaufmann (New York: Vintage, 1966).

Nietzsche, Friedrich, *Thus Spoke Zarathustra*, translated by Walter Kaufmann, in *The Portable Nietzsche* (New York: Viking, 1954).

Nietzsche, Friedrich, *The Dawn*, translated by Walter Kaufmann, in *The Portable Nietzsche* (New York: Viking, 1954).

Nietzsche, Friedrich, *The Gay Science*, translated by Walter Kaufmann (New York: Vintage, 1974).

Nietzsche, Friedrich, *On the Genealogy of Morals*, translated by Walter Kaufmann (New York: Vintage, 1969).

Nietzsche, Friedrich, *Twilight of the Idols*, translated by Walter Kaufmann, in *The Portable Nietzsche* (New York: Vintage, 1954).

There is extensive discussion of Nietzsche on punishment, revenge, and related issues in Michael Moore's "The Moral Worth of Retribution" and in my

"Moral Epistemology, the Retributive Emotions, and the 'Clumsy Moral Philosophy' of Jesus Christ." Nietzsche's thoughts on punishment are spread over various works, so I advise starting with Moore's essay.

Plato, *Republic*, translated by Robin Waterfield (Oxford: Oxford University Press, 1993).

Plato, *Laws*, translated by Trevor J. Saunders (New York: Penguin, 1975).

Rawls, John, *A Theory of Justice* (Cambridge, MA: Harvard University Press, 1971).

Richards, Norvin, "Forgiveness," *Ethics 99*, October 1988.

Rilke, Rainer Maria, "Autumn," in *The Book of Images*, translated by Edward Snow (New York: North Point Press, 1991).

Rorty, Richard, *Philosophy and Social Hope* (New York: Penguin, 1999).

Shaffer, Thomas J., "The Radical Reformation and the Jurisprudence of Forgiveness," in *Christian Perspectives on Legal Thought*, edited by Michael W. McConnel, Robert F. Cochran, and Angela C. Carmella (New Haven: Yale University Press, 2001).

Snow, Nancy, "Self-forgiveness," *Journal of Value Inquiry 27*, 1993.

Spinoza, Benedict, *Ethics*, translated by E. M. Curley (Princeton: Princeton University Press, 1985).

Tolstoy, Leo, "The Death of Ivan Ilych," translated by Louise and Aylmer Maude, in *Great Short Works of Leo Tolstoy* (New York: Harper and Row, 1967).

Trevor, William, *Felicia's Journey* (London: Viking, 1994).

Trevor, William, *Death in Summer* (New York: Viking, 1998).

Tutu, Bishop Desmond, *No Future Without Forgiveness* (New York: Doubleday, 1999). Bishop Tutu defined forgiveness as "waiving the right to revenge" in a PBS interview with Bill Moyers on April 27, 1999.

Weldon, Fay, *Female Friends* (London: Heinemann, 1975).

Williams, Bernard, *Shame and Necessity* (Berkeley: University of California Press, 1993).

Williams, Rowan, *A Ray of Darkness, Sermons and Reflections* (Cambridge, MA: Cowley Publications, 1995).

Wilson, A. N., *Incline our Hearts* (New York: Penguin, 1988).

Wisdom, John, "The Logic of 'God'," in *The Existence of God*, edited by John Hick (New York: Macmillan, 1964).

INDEX

abuse, 12, 15, 76, 79, 80, 82–83, 84, 85,
    116–17
Achilles, 17
actions
    character vs., 10
    moral values and, 107
Adam and Eve, 61, 62, 63
Adams, Marilyn, 90–92
Adams, Robert, 10, 12
addictions, 68
Agamemnon, 17
amends-making, 42–43, 83–84
American Southern Baptist Convention,
    39
amnesty, political, 15, 37
anger, 8
    forgiveness as overcoming, 59
    proper expression of, 38
    victim impact statements and, 27
    as vindictive emotion, 16, 17, 34
Anglicanism, 36
anxiety reduction, 75, 77, 79
apartheid, 15
Aquinas. *See* Thomas Aquinas
Argentina, 39–40
Aristotle, 6, 7, 11, 38
arrogance, 58, 84
Athena, 20

atonement
    Christian belief in, 112
    self-forgiveness following, 69–72
    See also penance
Auden, W. H., 91
Augustine, St., 35, 80, 96, 98, 100, 107
    "hate the sin . . . not the sinner" state-
        ment of, 35, 80
    punishment views of, 104–5, 109–10,
        112
Auschwitz, 44, 84
Austin, J. L., 54, 65
authentic guilt, 76, 84

Bacon, Lord, 71
battered women, 15, 80
betrayal, 12, 65, 117
*Between Vengeance and Forgiveness: Facing
    History after Genocide and Mass Vio-
    lence* (Minow), 5
Bible. *See* New Testament; Old Testa-
    ment; *specific books and gospels*
body. *See* soul/body dualism
Booth v. Maryland (1987), 28, 30, 31
Broad, C. D., 8
Buber, Martin, 76, 84
Bundy, Ted, 33
Bush, George W., 4, 98

Butler, Joseph, 12–13, 18–19, 21, 22, 38, 58, 66, 77, 101, 104

capital punishment, 4, 107
 as brutalizing, 45–46
 Christian beliefs and, 95–96, 98, 101, 109–13
 Christian defense of, 97–98, 109
 Christian tensions with, 100, 112–13
 effects on soul of, 99
 as impeding repentance and rebirth, 112
 as last resort, 109–10, 112
 public responses to, 21
Capote, Truman, vii
Capra, Frank, 98
Carroll, Lewis, 7
Catechism of the Catholic Church, 106, 112
categorical imperative, 62
Catholic Church, 39, 105–6, 112
"Catholicism and Capital Punishment" (Dulles), 105–6
character
 actions vs., 10
 community values and, 54
 elements of evil and, 10–11
 forgiveness as moral virtue of, 13
 human fallibility and, 88
 just deserts and, 106
 Kantian vs. Aristotelian view of, 11
 mistakes in judging, 108–9
 punishment's effects on, 45, 99–100, 105, 106–7
 repentance and, 42–43
 self-hatred from weaknesses of, 68
 See also deep character; inner character
character retributivism, 43, 44, 45, 50–51, 52, 106–8
cheap grace, 71–72
child abuse, 12, 76, 84, 85
China, 46
Chirac, Jacques, 39
Christianity, 87–93, 95–113
 capital punishment and, 95, 96, 97–98, 100, 101, 109–13
 forgiveness as central virtue of, ix, 8, 76, 79, 80, 87–88, 91–92, 111, 115

forgiveness assumptions in, 81
 interpretations of forgiveness commands in, 71, 88
 love's centrality in, 8, 80, 97, 98, 100–101
 rejection of vindictive passions by, 20–21
 repentance prior to forgiveness and, 88, 91
 retributive punishment and, 104, 105–6
 summary of punishment views of, 111–12
 unconditional forgiveness and, 35–36, 88
 vengeance teachings of, 21, 88–90, 106
City of God, The (Augustine), 109
civil disobedience, 46
class bias, 31
Clinton, Bill, 103
closure, 27, 104
Coetzee, J. M., 37
Cohen, Hermann, 110
collective repentance, 39–40, 54–56, 101
common good, 104–5, 111, 112
common sense, 21–22, 29
community
 Christian view of punishment and, 99–100
 collective repentance and, 54
 criminal responsibility and, 54
 Jewish view of forgiveness and, 81
 reintegration of repentant criminals into, 53–54
 values of, 48–50, 52, 54
community service, 48
compassion, 13–14
 criminal justice and, 27
 linked with forgiveness and mercy, 39, 55
conciliatory spirit, 102
condescension, 84
confession, 15
Constitution, U.S., 28
contempt, 59
Corinthians, First Letter of Paul to the, 97

counseling. *See* forgiveness counseling; psychotherapy
"Counseling within the Forgiveness Triad: On Forgiving, Receiving Forgiveness, and Self-Forgiveness" (Enright), 74
courage, 9
cowardice, 9
criminal justice
  character and, 45
  Christianity and, 95–113
  collective repentance and, 39–40, 54–56, 101
  commitment of moral horrors and, 12
  cruelty rationalized as, 33–34, 89, 103, 111
  forgiveness boosterism and, 116
  as institutionalized revenge, 20
  intention and, 88, 107
  luck as element in, 28–29, 30
  mercy vs. forgiveness and, 14
  overcriminalization and, 45–46
  reentry problems and, 53–54
  repentance's place in, 40, 50–56
  responsible agent and, 13
  retributive punishment and, 3–4, 17, 29, 57, 104
  self-deception and, 103, 104, 107–8, 111
  self-defense justification and, 13
  victim impact statements and, 4, 27–31
  vindictiveness and, 27–31, 54–55
  See also capital punishment; punishment; retributive punishment; rule of law
"cruel and unusual punishment" stricture, 28, 104
cruelty
  evil character linked with, 10, 107
  penal practices and, 101, 112
  self-righteous vindictiveness and, 14, 33–34, 89, 103, 111
"culture of victims", 40
Cure of Troy, The (Heaney), 92–93

Darrow, Clarence, 96
Dead Man Walking (film), 99–100

Death of Ivan Ilych (Tolstoy), 99
death penalty. *See* capital punishment
debt, forgiveness of, 15
deep character
  definition of, 88
  relevance to criminal justice, 45
deep character retributivism, 106–8
defiance theory of immorality, 60–66, 69
degradation of victim, 43, 44, 77, 78
delusional psychosis, 11
democracy, 28
Denning, Lord, 97
depression reduction, 79
deserts
  definitions of, 106
  retribution and, 42, 43, 51, 85, 105–6, 111
deterrence, punishment as, 17, 42, 43, 45, 50, 52
Deuteronomy, Book of, 98
"dirty war" (Argentina), 40
disappointment, 3, 59
Disgrace (Coetzee), 37
disobedience, 63
Doctorow, E. L., 24
Doctrine of Right, The (Kant), 102, 103
Doctrine of Virtue, The (Kant), 102, 105
Donatists, 109–10
Dostoevsky, Fyodor, 60
due process, 20, 28
Duff, R. A., 45, 48–49, 105
Dulles, Avery Cardinal, 105–6
duty, 61
Dworkin, Ronald, 111

egalitarianism, 30, 31, 104
ego ideal, 60
egoism, 66
Eichmann, Adolph, 12, 85
Eighth Amendment (U.S. Constitution), 28
emotions
  forgiveness as overcoming negative, 59
  intellectual belief vs. feeling of, 19
  justice and, 14, 33, 103
  rational vs. irrational, 22, 23

emotions (*continued*)
vindictive, 16, 17–18. *See also* vindictiveness
Enright, Robert D., 73, 74, 76–77, 78,
79, 80, 81, 83–84
envy, 14
equality *See* egalitarianism; inequality
equal protection, 28, 104
Essays on Philosophical Counseling
(Lahav), 75
eternal life. *See* salvation
ethics theories, 6, 7–8
ethnic cleansing, 10, 84
Eumenides ("Kindly Ones"), 20
Evangelium Vitae (1995 encyclical), 112
evil
balanced view of vindictive passions
and, 38
Christian faith and, 92
Christian view of punishment and,
111
clarification of term, 9–12
existential (authentic) guilt and, 76, 84
forgiveness counseling and, 85
God's children and, 91–92
human fallibility and, 89
human responsibility for, 11
as irrevocable, 85
Judeo-Christian tradition on origin
of, 61
Kant's view of, 61, 100
madness and, 11
Nietzsche's warning about punishment and, 14, 88, 89, 100, 103, 111
paradigms of, 12–13
passions of, 18, 21
retribution for, 85
self-forgiveness for, 76, 84
self-hatred vs. self-forgiveness for,
84–85
universal prescriptions of forgiveness
and, 81–83
values and, 11–12, 75–76
vengeance and, 89
victim's choice of responses to, 3, 76
See also sin
excuse, definition of, 13

execution. *See* capital punishment
existential (authentic) guilt, 76, 84
external actions, 13, 81, 101
Ezekiel, Book of, 113

faith, 92
fallibility, 88, 89, 90, 91
feeling. *See* emotions; inner feeling
Felicia's Journey (Trevor), 89, 91
Fields, W. C., 99
films, 21, 24, 98, 99
Fingarette, Herbert, 47
forgiveness
acceptance of, 76
as act of arrogance, 58
balanced view of, ix, 33–38
blessings gained from, 34
boosterism about, viii, 74, 78, 116
cautions about, viii, ix, 19, 77–78,
81–83, 115–16
choice between vindictiveness and,
116
Christian case for, ix, 8, 34–36, 76, 79,
80, 81, 87–93, 111, 115
Christian interpretations of, 71
Christian love linked with, 100–101
Christian vs. Jewish core virtue of, 81
clarification of term, 9–12
compassion linked with, 39, 55
competing tensions and, 8
conditional vs. unconditional, 36, 81.
See also repentance
confusion with other responses, 13–14
counseling of. *See* forgiveness counseling
defining meaning of, 7
definitions of, 12–13, 15, 58–59
difficulty of, 115–16
effects on wrongdoer of, 58
Enright's triad of, 76–77, 84–85
of evildoers, 3, 76
evil horrors as obstacles to, 11–12
free gift of, 71
further victimization from, 80
group, 5, 6, 15–16
as internal change vs. external behavior, 13, 81, 101

interpersonal vs. group, 5
Jewish conditions for, 81
love and, 8, 80, 84, 86
mercy vs., 13–14, 39, 55
nature of, 12–13
New Testament parables and, 34–35, 88, 96, 101–2
opiate function of, 80
other responses to wrongdoing vs., 13–14
as overcoming resentment, 58
popular interest in, viii, 74
problems with hasty/uncritical, 19, 20, 77–78, 115–16
psychotherapy and, 48, 72, 73–86, 116
punishment's compatibility with, 95, 100–101
reasons for, 57–58
receipt of, 83–84
reconciliation distinguished from, 80
reconciliation without, 14–16, 37
repentance as opening door to, 43–44
repentance's sincerity as basis of, 35, 36–37, 70–71, 80, 81, 82–83, 95
without repentance, 70–71, 81, 82–83
of self. See self-forgiveness
self-hatred and, 68–69
self-respect and, 58, 77–79, 92
skepticism about universal prescriptions for, 81–83
tension with vengeance, 3, 4, 5, 8
unconditional, 35–36
victim impact statements vs., 4
vindictive passions vs., 16
as virtue, ix, 6, 8, 13, 33–38, 81
Forgiveness and Mercy (Murphy and Hampton), viii, 25, 57, 58
forgiveness counseling, 73–86, 116–17
for evil clients, 85
goods promised by, 79
questions raised by, 79–80, 85–86
forgiveness triad, components of, 76–77, 84–85
Fourteenth Amendment (U.S. Constitution), 28
France, 39
freedom, responsibility with, 107

free riding, 106
free will, 11
Freud, Sigmund, 60, 75
fundamentalism, 97
Furies, 20

Garland, Bonnie, 69
Gaylin, Willard, 69–70
Geach, Peter, 19, 91
gender differences, 3
genocide, 10, 40
Georgia, state penal code, 46
Germany, 39, 73, 409. See also Nazis
getting even. See vengeance; vindictiveness
God
eternal soul and, 99
forgiveness commandment of, 91
forgiveness of human sin by, 91
human creation in image of, 78, 91–92
love of and for, 92, 96, 97, 98, 104
moral authority of, 62, 63, 107, 111
vengeance and, 88
grace, 97, 100, 107, 112
forgiveness as act of, 71
Greco, El, 98
grievance retributivism, 43, 50–51
Groundwork of the Metaphysics of Morals (Kant), 107
group forgiveness, reconciliation and, 5, 6, 15–16
group repentance, 39–40
Grundlegung (Kant), 107
guilt
of Adam and Eve, 63
authentic (existential) vs. neurotic, 76, 84
about not forgiving, 82
punishment and, 102
repentance and, 46–47
about revenge-seeking, 4
despite self-forgiveness, 70
self-hatred and, 60
of survivor, 66–67, 68
wrongful defiance and, 63–64
guilt morality, shame morality vs., 63
Gyges' ring, 90

Haber, Joram Graf, 77
Hamlet (Shakespeare), 112
Hampton, Jean, viii, 25, 45, 57–71, 74, 106
happiness, 75
Harding, Tonya, 53
Hare, John, 107
Häring, Bernard, 97
harms. *See* wrongdoing
Hart, Herbert, 6
"hate the sin, not the sinner" (Augustine), 35, 80
hatred, 10, 14, 18
    cautions on punishment based on, 102–3, 104, 111
    forgiveness as overcoming, 59, 101
    resentment distinguished from, 104
    vengeance and, 89
    as vindictive emotion, 16, 17
    See also moral hatred; self-hatred
healing, forgiveness as, 34
Heaney, Seamus, 92–93
Hebrews, Letter to the, 102
Herrin, Richard, 69–70
Hijuelos, Oscar, 55–56
Hill, Tom, 77
Holmes, Oliver Wendell, Jr., 63
Holmgren, Margaret, 77, 78, 80
Holocaust, 39, 44, 66, 83, 84
homicide. *See* murder
homosexuality, 46
Honorius, emperor of Rome, 109–10
Horney, Karen, 23, 33
Hotel New Hampshire, The (Irving), 25
Human Development Study Group (University of Wisconsin, Madison), 74
human fallibility, 88, 89, 90, 91
human soul, 47, 98–99
Hume, David, vii–viii
humility, 85, 88, 111
hurt, 3, 44
hypocrisy, 88, 89

Iliad (Homer), 17
immorality, defiance theory of, 60–66, 69
incest survivors, 79, 82–83
Incline Our Hearts (Wilson), 64–65

indifference, 59
individual repentance, 40
inequality
    "getting even" and perception of, 25
    between victim and wrongdoer, 35, 43, 47, 77, 81
    victim impact statements and, 30, 31, 104
inner character, judgments of, 106–9, 110, 111
inner feeling, forgiveness linked with, 13, 107
insanity
    evil and, 11
    revenge-taking portrayed as, 24–25
insanity defense, 13
intention, 88, 107
internal changes, 13, 88, 101
interpersonal forgiveness. *See* forgiveness
Irving, John, 25
Israel, 73

jails. *See* prisons and jails
Japan, 39, 40
Japanese Americans, wartime internment of, 40
jealousy, 18
Jesus, 89, 90, 91, 97
    eternal life and, 99
    love of God and, 98
    parables of, 34–35, 88, 96, 101–2
    words from the cross, 36
Jews. *See* Holocaust; Judaism; Old Testament
John, Gospel According to, 88, 89, 98, 106
John Paul, Pope, 39
Johnson, Samuel, 45, 99, 112
Judaism
    love commandment and, 98
    repentance-based forgiveness and, 81
Judeo-Christian tradition, 3, 61. *See also* Christianity; Judaism
Judy, Steven, 20
just deserts. *See* deserts
justice
    Christian love vs., 97
    imprecise use of term, 9

as rationalization for other emotions,
14, 33, 103
vengeance differentiated from, 4
See also criminal justice; punishment
justification, definition of, 13
juvenile offenders, 49–50

Kant, Immanuel, 9, 11, 20, 42, 90, 96
capital punishment advocacy by, 110
on compassion and law, 27
deep character retributivism and, 107
defense of retributive punishment by,
100, 102, 103, 105, 106
doctrine of radical freedom and responsibility, 107
on immorality, 61, 62, 63, 64, 66
on self-deception, 108
on servility, 20
Kerrigan, Nancy, 53
Kierkegaard, Søren, 41, 92, 98
Kleist, Heinrich von, 24
Kohlhaas, Michael (fictional character),
24, 33

Lahav, Ran, 75
law. *See* criminal justice; moral law;
punishment; rule of law
Laws (Plato), 45
legal justice. *See* criminal justice; rule of
law
Leviticus, Book of, 98
literature
revenge portrayals, 24, 25, 33
self-help and recovery, viii, 74
See also specific titles
Living Bible, The, 106
Loeb and Leopold case, 86
Lord's Prayer, 36
love
Christian valuation of, 8, 80, 95, 97,
98, 100–101
criminal punishment and, 96–98,
102–3, 104, 111
forgiveness as outgrowth of, 8, 80, 84,
86
value of God's, 92
luck, 28–29, 30, 64, 90
Luke, Gospel According to, 36, 91, 98

Luther, Martin, 116

madness. *See* insanity
Maher, Bill, 9
malice, 14
Mandela, Nelson, 6
Manson, Charles, 11
Mao Tse-tung, 46
Marcellinus, 109–10
Marx, Karl, 80
Matthew, Gospel According to, 34–35,
91, 99, 101, 102, 105
Maxwell, William, 65, 66
Measure for Measure (Shakespeare), 103
Mengele, Joseph, 83
mens rea, 88, 107
mercy
compassion and, 39, 55
degrees of, 52
forgiveness vs., 13–14, 39, 55
repentance's effects on, 39, 50–51, 52,
54
self-deception and, 103
Michael Kohlhaas (von Kleist), 24, 33
Milton, John, 61
Minow, Martha, 5
Misérables, Les (Hugo), 71, 80, 84
Montaigne, Michel de, 41, 108
Moore, Michael, 70, 89, 106
moral failures, 60, 65
moral gap, 107
moral hatred
definition of, 59–60
of self, 59, 60, 64, 66, 72
moral horrors. *See* evil
moral humility, 85
moral introspection, 90
moral law, 61, 62, 63, 65–66
moral luck, 28–29, 30, 64
moral values
capital punishment and, 96
Christian influence on, 96. *See also*
Christianity
communitarian, 48–50, 54, 52
competition among, 4, 7
defiance of, 60–62, 63–64
emotional commitment and, 19
evil practices and, 11–12, 85

moral values (*continued*)
forgiveness as, ix, 3, 76–77, 87
forgiveness as possible compromise to, 19, 77–78, 115–16
forgiveness counseling and, 85–86
forgiveness for good of society as, 15
gap between knowing and doing and, 107
human compliance with, 90
legitimacy of vindictiveness and, 17–18, 19, 20–21
of love vs. justice, 97
in psychotherapy, 76
in punishment, 116
repentance and, 42–43, 55–56
resentment as defender of, 19, 104, 115
retributivism and, 106
shame and, 60
shame vs. guilt and, 63
vindictiveness and, 17–21
moral virtues. *See* virtue
"Moral Worth of Retribution, The" (Moore), 89–90, 106
Morris, Herbert, 45, 66, 106
Mr. Ives' Christmas (Hijuelos), 55–56
murder, 10, 29, 30, 53, 107
Murdoch, Iris, 7
My Little Chickadee (film), 99

Native Americans, 40
Nazis, 12, 39, 44, 68, 76, 84, 85
neighbor, love of, 96, 98
Netherlands, 73
Neu, Jerome, 18
neurotic guilt, 76
neurotics, 23
goal of psychotherapy for, 75, 77
New Testament, 47, 106
parables, 34–35, 84–85, 96, 101–2
unconditional forgiveness and, 36
Nietzsche, Friedrich, 7, 23, 34, 108
on misguided punishment, 14, 88, 89, 100, 103, 111
nonmoral guilt, 66
nonviolence, 46

O'Connor, Flannery, 98
Oedipus, 60
offender. *See* wrongdoer
"Of Repentance" (Montaigne), 108
Old Testament, 61, 62, 63, 106
capital punishment and, 97, 98, 113
Omar Khayyam, 86
"On Forgiveness of Injuries" (Butler), 12–13
Oresteia trilogy (Aeschylus), 20
Ozick, Cynthia, 44, 84

parables, 34–35, 88, 96, 101–2
Paradise Lost (Milton), 61
pardons
issue of deep character and, 45
Kant's skepticism about, 103
victim impact statements and, 27
parole
issue of deep character and, 45
rights restoration and, 53
victim impact statements and, 27
passions. *See* emotions
paternalistic theory of punishment, 45–49, 50
Paul, St., 47, 97, 102
Payne v. Tennessee (1991), 30
pedophile priests, 39
penance, 47, 48
Penn, Sean, 99–100
Perelman, S. J., ix, 19
perpetrator. *See* wrongdoer
personal failures, self-hatred from, 68
personality types, 8, 19–20. *See also* character
pettiness, 33
philosophical counseling, 73–86
forgiveness of others and, 77–86
questions raised by, 75–77, 85–86
philosophy
Butler's essay on forgiveness and, 12–13
clarification of terms in, 9–10
Kantian vs. Aristotelian, 11
personal element in, 7–8
rationality as intrinsic to, 73, 75, 76–77
value of, 6–7

views on punishment, 96
See also worldview; *specific philosophers*
Plato, 45, 47, 90
plea bargains, 53
Posner, Richard A., 54–55
Powell, Lewis, 28, 30
power
    vindictiveness and, 25
    of wrongdoer, 35, 43, 47, 77, 81
    See also inequality
Prager, Dennis, 109
pride, 91
prisons and jails
    bad conditions in, 34
    as brutalizing factor, 45, 55, 105
    expression of Christian love and,
        102–3, 104
    faith-based programs, 105
    as "penitentiaries", 40, 48
    sentencing to, 4, 50
psychotherapy, 48, 72, 73–86, 88
    forgiveness boosterism in, 75, 116–17
    forgiveness of others as value in,
        77–84
    general goal of, 74–75
    philosophical rationality and, 77
    values and, 76
    See also forgiveness counseling
punishment
    aim or purpose of, 41–42, 103–4
    ancient Greek justification for, 20
    for as common good, 104–5, 111, 112
    callous indifference and, 101–2
    Catholic catechism on, 106
    character retributivism and, 43, 44,
        45, 50–51, 52, 106–8
    Christianity and, 95–113
    Christian views summarized, 111–12
    communitarian view of, 48–49, 52
    constitutional constraints on, 28
    as deterrence, 17, 42, 43, 45, 50, 52
    eternal life and, 98–99
    forgiveness and, 95, 100–101
    grievance retributivism and, 43, 50–51
    human knowledge and, 88–89
    justifications of, 42, 102
    love and, 96–98, 102–3, 104, 111

luck as element in, 28–29
    as moral improvement, 45, 47
    as necessary evil, 111
    Nietzsche's warning on, 14, 88, 89,
        100, 103, 111
    official discretion and, 50
    paternalistic theory of, 45–49, 50
    as penance, 47, 48
    relationship of repentance with, 40,
        41–42, 45–47, 48, 50–51
    as retributive. *See* retributive punishment
    self-deceptive leniency and, 103
    severity based on actual harm, 30
    spiritual transformation from, 105, 111
    unacceptable types of, 104
    unjustness and, 46
    values served by, 116
    as vengeance, 4, 20. *See also*
        vengeance
    victim's influence on, 14, 17–18
    wrongdoing as focus of, 44–45
purity of heart, 81
Purity of Heart (Kierkegaard), 41

racism, 18, 39
radical evil, 11
Ragtime (Doctorow), 24
rape, 10, 12, 43, 47, 85, 104
rationality
    philosophical, 73, 75, 76–77
    of vindictiveness, 17–18
Rawls, John, 79, 90, 96
"reactive attitude" of resentment, 19
rebirth (spiritual transformation)
    Christian belief in, 112
    from free gift of forgiveness, 71, 80,
        84
    from punishment, 105, 111
    repentance and, 99–100
Rechtslehre (Kant), 102, 103
reconciliation
    change in inner feeling prior to, 13,
        81
    with evildoers, 3
    forgiveness and, 5, 13, 14–15
    forgiveness distinguished from, 80

reconciliation (*continued*)
  forgiveness without, 14, 15–16
  sincere repentance as step toward,
    36–37
religion. *See* Christianity; God; Judaism;
    Judeo-Christian tradition; moral
    values
Religion Within the Limits of Reason Alone
    (Kant), 61, 90, 107, 108
religious right, 97
remorse, repentance and, 41, 42–43
repentance, 39–56
  character retributivism and, 42–43,
    50–51
  Christian belief in, 112
  as Christian precondition for forgive-
    ness, 88, 91
  coerced vs. sincere, 37
  collective, 39–40, 54–56, 101
  counterfeit, 108
  criminal justice and, 40, 50–56
  decreased valuation of, 40
  definition of, 41
  forgiveness based on sincerity of, 35,
    36–37, 58, 78, 80, 81, 82–83, 95
  forgiveness without, 70–71, 81, 82–83
  from free gift of forgiveness, 71
  group, 39–40
  as interior act, 41
  as Jewish precondition for forgiveness,
    81
  moral elements of, 42–43, 55–56
  opening door to forgiveness, 43–44
  prospect of death and, 99–100
  punishment as generating, 45–46,
    50–51
  reintegration into community and,
    53–54, 81
  for self-forgiveness, 69–72
  sincerity of, 108–9
  social dimension of, 41
  suffering and, 46–47, 51–52
Republic (Plato), 90
resentment
  as adaptive strategy, 82
  amends making and, 84
  defense of, 18, 77, 78, 82–83, 104, 115
  forgiveness as overcoming, 58, 59
  moral values defended by, 19, 104, 115
  purpose of, 104, 115
  reactive attitude of, 19
  self-respect linked with, 18, 19–20,
    77, 78
  as vindictive emotion, 16, 17, 18, 115
responsibility
  collective, 40
  deep character retributivism and,
    106–7
  evil and, 11
  repentance as remorseful acceptance
    of, 41
  of wrongdoer, 40
responsible agent, 13
ressentiment, 14, 23, 103
restitution, 48
retribution
  of character, 43, 44, 45, 50–51, 52, 88,
    106–8
  Christian view of punishment and,
    104, 105–6
  concept of deserts and, 29, 42, 43, 44,
    51, 85, 105–6, 111
  grievance vs. character, 43
  Plato's view of, 45
  repentance and, 43, 44, 50–51
  role in punishment. *See* retributive
    punishment
retributive punishment, 45, 57
  in criminal law, 3–4, 17
  deterrence vs., 42
  imprecise use of term, 9, 105–6
  Kant's defense of, 100, 102, 103, 105,
    106, 110
  mercy vs. forgiveness and, 14
  as proportional to desert, 29, 42, 111
  as vengeance, 17
  victim satisfaction and, 104
  See also capital punishment
revenge-taking. *See* vengeance
Richards, Norvin, 59
Rilke, Rainer Maria, 92
Robbins, Tim, 99
Romans, Letter of Paul to the, 47, 88,
    89, 106
Rorty, Richard, 6–7
Royko, Mike, 21

rule of law, 4, 20
  Christian values and, 104–5
  reasons for compliance with, 90
  resentment as defense of, 104
  tragic worldview and, 100
  victim satisfaction balanced with due
    process and, 20
  See also criminal justice; punishment

sadism, 33–34
sadness, 59
salvation, 97, 98–99, 100, 105, 112
Samuel, First Book of, 106
Sartre, Jean-Paul, 83
Scalia, Antonin, 28–29, 30
self-deception, 14, 89, 103, 104, 107–8,
  111
self-defense, 13, 18, 19, 115
self-esteem, 79. *See also* self-respect
self-forgiveness, 57–72
  concept of, 58–59
  counseling for, 74
  easy and unearned, 71–72
  by evildoers, 76, 84
  example of shallow, 70
  in forgiveness triad, 76, 84–85
  repentance and atonement prior to,
    69–72
  self-hatred and, 59, 60, 64, 69, 72
self-hatred
  bringing evildoers to, 84–85
  degrees of, 68
  from doing right thing, 67
  from failures of virtue, 68, 72
  forgiveness of others and, 68–69
  from harm inflicted on others, 64–65,
    72
  moral failings and, 66
  self-forgiveness and, 59, 60, 64, 69, 72
  shame and, 65
  sincere repentance and, 51
  survivor guilt and, 66
self-help books, viii, 74
self-honesty, 90
self-importance, 91, 92
self-interest, 10, 43
selfishness, 66
self-loathing. *See* self-hatred

self-respect
  forgiveness as compromising, ix, 58,
    77–79, 92
  forgiveness based on repentance and,
    80
  forgiveness counseling and, 79
  forgiveness while maintaining, 58, 78,
    92
  juvenile offenders and, 49–50
  religious vs. secular sources of, 78–79
  resentment linked with, 18, 19–20, 77,
    78
  vindictive emotions and, 23, 115
  wrongdoer as compromising, 35
self-righteousness, 14, 33–34, 89, 103,
  111
sensations, emotions vs., 22
sentencing. *See* criminal justice
September 11, 2001, attacks, 4, 9
servility, 5, 19, 20, 77–78
sexual abuse, 12, 76, 82–83
Shaffer, Thomas J., 100–101
Shakespeare, William, 103, 112
shame, 60, 63–64, 65, 70
Shame and Necessity (Williams), 63
shame morality, guilt morality vs., 63
Silverado (film), 21
Simpson, O. J., 52, 53
sin
  Augustine on, 35, 80, 100
  Christian perspective on, 88, 91
  Kant on, 100
  moral introspection and, 89–90
  See also evil
skepticism, philosophical, 75
slavery, 39, 40
Snow, Nancy, 59, 67
social control, 43
Socrates, 107
Socratic method, 6–7
sodomy, 46
So Long, See You Tomorrow (Maxwell), 65
soul/body dualism, 47
  Christian view of punishment and,
    98–99
South African Truth and Reconciliation
  Commission, 5, 15–16, 37
Spinoza, Benedict, 23

spiritual transformation. *See* rebirth
spite, 14
Stoicism, 20
Strawson, Peter, 19, 77
suffering
    Christian view of, 91, 101
    punishment as infliction of, 41–42,
        47, 48
    repentance and, 46–47, 51–52
    theory of deserved, 51, 111
    undeserved, 108
    vindictive emotions causing, 17
    vindictive emotions resulting from,
        117
Sunflower, The (Wiesenthal), 44
Supreme Court, U.S., 28–30, 64
survivor guilt, 66–67, 68

"Ted Bundy Memorial Barbecue", 33
Temple, William, 97
Teresa, Mother, 108
Theory of Justice, A (Rawls), 79
therapy. *See* psychotherapy
Thomas Aquinas, 96, 104, 1105
thoughtlessness, 66
threats, 43
Tlingit culture, 49–50
toleration, 9
Tolstoy, Leo, 99
torture, 3, 10, 12, 84, 104
tragic worldview, 100
Trevor, William, 89, 91
Truth and Reconciliation Commission
    (South Africa), 5, 15–16, 37
Tugendlehre (Kant), 102, 105
Tutu, Desmond, 15
twelve-step programs, 84
Tyson, Mike, 52, 53

"unforgiving servant" parable, 34–35, 88,
    101–2
University of Wisconsin, Madison, 74
"Upon Resentment" (Butler sermon),
    18–19, 104
utilitarianism, 60

Valjean, Jean (fictional character), 71, 80,
    84

values. *See* moral values
vengeance
    central Christian teachings on, 88–90,
        106
    Christian negative view of, 21
    common-sense beliefs about, 21–22
    criminal punishment as, 31
    definition of, 17
    depicted as insanity, 24–25
    depicted as self-defeating, 25
    goal of, 17, 89
    hypocrisy and, 89
    imprecise use of term, 9
    justice differentiated from, 4
    media popularity of, 21, 24
    moderate and proportional, 24, 33
    retribution and, 57
    rule of law as institutionalization of,
        4, 20, 31
    sense of superiority and, 25
    tension with forgiveness, 3, 4, 5, 8
    as tit-for-tat scorekeeping, 33
    by victim of evil, 3
    vindictive passions and, 16, 17, 23,
        25–26
    See also vindictiveness
victim impact statements, 4, 27–31, 64
victims
    closure and, 27, 104
    community assumption of personae
        of, 20
    degradation of, 35, 43, 44, 77, 78
    egalitarian treatment of, 30
    grievance retributivism and, 43, 50–51
    hasty forgiveness and acceptance of
        status of, 79–80, 117
    input into criminal punishment by, 14
    institutionalization of vindictiveness
        and, 20
    repentance as opening to forgiveness
        by, 43–44, 53
    responses to serious wrongs by, 3, 6
    shame morality and, 63
    symbolic harm to, 77–78
    vindictive emotions felt by, 17, 18–19,
        117
    vindictive satisfaction of, 17, 104
    wrongdoers' power over, 35, 43, 47,

77, 81
wrongdoers seen as, 40, 54, 116
victim satisfaction
complexity of issue, 104
rule of law and, 20
victims' rights movement
criminal punishment and, 14
European vs. American view of, 4
See also victim impact statements
Vidal, Gore, vii
vigilante activity, 20, 21, 24
vindictiveness, 17–26
appraisal of arguments against, 21–25,
31
balanced view of, 20–21, 33, 38
as buffer against being wronged,
19–20
case for, 18–19
choice between reason and, 116
Christian challenge to, 20–21, 89
class bias in condemnation of, 31
complexity of, 31
in criminal justice system, 3, 14,
17–18, 27–31, 54–55
dangers of, 31
feeling vs. acting on, 25–26
institutionalization of, 20
legitimacy of, 115
moral status of, 17–18, 19, 20–21
passions of, 16, 17–18
as personality trait, 8
power as element in, 25
proportional acts of, 24
respect for victim's emotions of, 117
self-righteous, 14, 33–34, 89, 103, 111
victim impact statements and, 27–31
victim rights' movement and, 4, 14
by victims of evil, 3
See also vengeance
virtue
as character state, 11, 42–43
forgiveness as, ix, 6, 8, 13, 33–38, 81
love as, 97
mercy as, 13–14, 39
reconciliation and, 15–16
repentance as, 41
resentment and, 19
self-hatred from failures of, 68

self-loathing from lack of, 68
self-respect as, 77
vindictiveness and, 18, 26

war, 9
Washington state, 49
weakness, 66
Weldon, Fay, vii, ix, 92
White, Byron, 28–29, 30
Wiesel, Elie, 44, 84
Wiesenthal, Simon, 44
Williams, Bernard, 63
Williams, Rowan, 115
Wills, Garry, 98
Wilson, A. N., 64–65, 66
Wisdom, John, 6
worldview
evil and, 11–12, 76, 85
hasty forgiveness linked with morally
flabby, 115
philosophical skepticism and, 75
tragic, 100
World War II, 39, 40, 67
wrongdoer
forgiveness and rebirth of, 71, 80
forgiveness as good for, 58, 69, 70–71
forgiveness without repentance of,
70–71, 81, 82–83
luck's role in justified punishment of,
29
mistakes of hasty forgiveness of, 115
power over victim by, 35, 43, 47, 77,
81
reasons for forgiveness of, 57–58
repentance by, 42–43, 50–52, 58,
69–72, 78, 80
repentance prior to forgiveness of, 91
resentment of forgiveness by, 58
unrepentance of, 52, 70–71, 72
value of punishment for, 116
vengeance against, 89
victim status of, 40, 54, 116
See also self-forgiveness
wrongdoing
Christian punishment of, 95–113
as communicative act, 77
degrading message of, 35, 43, 44, 47,
77

wrongdoing (*continued*)
    distinction between mercy and for-
        giveness and, 14
    justification of resentment of, 19
    malicious infliction of, 12
    moral categories of, 10
    ordinary vs. evil, 84–85. *See also* evil
    politically motivated, 15
    responses to, 3, 13–14, 19, 44
    self-forgiveness for, 69, 72
    self-hatred from, 64, 64–69

severity of punishment based on actu-
    ality of, 30
soul/body dualism and, 47
vindictive passions as deterrent of,
    19–20
vindictive passions as motivation for,
    18
vindictive passions as response to, 16,
    22–23

Yoder, John Howard, 100